O N T A R I O ' S
HERITAGE QUILTS

Marilyn I. Walker

Stoddart

A BOSTON MILLS PRESS BOOK

Canadian Cataloguing in Publication Data

Walker, Marilyn I. (Marilyn Isabelle), 1934-
    Ontario's heritage quilts

Includes bibliographical references.
ISBN 1-55046-066-8

1. Quilts - Ontario - History. I. Title.

NK9113.A3068 1992   746.9'7   C92-093912-0

First published in 1992 by
Stoddart Publishing Co. Limited,
34 Lesmill Road,
Toronto, Canada
M3B 2T6

A BOSTON MILLS PRESS BOOK
The Boston Mills Press
132 Main Street
Erin, Ontario
N0B 1T0

Winners of the
Heritage Canada
Communications Award

American Association
for State and Local History
Award Winner

Edited by Noel Hudson
Design by Gillian Stead
Typeset by Lincoln Graphics Inc., St. Catharines, Ontario
Photography by Shades of Light, Niagara Falls, Ontario
Printed in Hong Kong
By Book Art Inc., Toronto

The publisher gratefully acknowledges the support of the Canada Council
the Ontario Arts Council and the Ontario Publishing Centre in the
development of writing and publishing in Canada.

CONTENTS

FOREWORD

Quilts are an important facet of the economic and social history of Ontario, and as such are significant and fragile historical artifacts. Until the late nineteenth century all homes, from the manor to that of the hired hand, contained quilts. Quilts were utilitarian objects which reflected the lives of women—their joys, their sorrows, time stolen from their long and demanding days; quilting was their relaxation as well as their therapy. Since quilts were created by women and therefore looked upon as ordinary household works, they were given no recognition in the annals of history. The purpose of this book is to introduce Ontario's pioneer quilters and their artistic creations to general readers, history buffs, and current and succeeding generations of quilt aficionados.

An antiquarian craze is currently sweeping the country. In an increasingly multicultural, technology-oriented society, our populace longs for that which is familiar. Nothing evokes the past quite like a heritage quilt.

Quilts were generally functional objects; they were not given any special care. Hence many have succumbed to the ravages of wear, climate and vermin. However, we are fortunate that many have survived. Most of the ones shown in this book are in family collections and have not been exhibited publicly.

I have endeavoured to provide the reader with an overview of quilts in Ontario; this book is not meant to be an in-depth study of any one technique or design. Many of the designs will be recognizable to the quilt historian. The nineteenth-century quilter took great pride in perpetuating

domestic art. Quilting gave her the freedom to work with a familiar pattern and just change the "set" or the sashing. It must be remembered that the artist-craftswoman never expected that a century or more later an audience would be judging her work on its artistic merits. However, pioneer women used their most interesting fabric scraps to add some colour to their dull, drab and often depressing homes. Quilting provided these busy women an opportunity for creative expression. This book pays tribute to Ontario's pioneer women who instilled in succeeding generations a love for "fabric art" while simultaneously providing one of the necessities of life.

It is difficult, if not impossible, to date many quilts accurately if nothing is known about them by their owners. However, assisted by textile conservators and existing literature, I have attempted to date some of the quilts in this book. Notwithstanding, the date attached to a quilt can only be considered an estimate, as many of these quilts were created using scrap fabrics. Some fabrics may be at least 25 years older than the quilt on which they appear. Fortunately, many of the quilts have been passed from generation to generation and, assisted by family records, many owners were able to date their possessions.

Four years were spent on research and development of this book, as I chose for my criteria quilts that are *not* in public museums. What is the heritage of Ontario, who were the people who made these quilts, and what were their backgrounds, were the principal questions to be answered by this research. Many people took the time to personally

research their family's history and share this information with me. The owners of the quilts all very graciously loaned their treasures in order that they could be photographed in suitable environments. This was a monumental feat of logistics, moving large numbers of quilts around the province. However, with the help of many friends and of guild members in each city, this was accomplished with no loss of or damage to any of these family artifacts.

While I, as the author, assumed the role of facilitator, I was very fortunate to have a nucleus of artistic friends who assisted me in choosing the quilts and the room layouts. Recognizing that you, the reader, may like to study and examine some quilts in detail, I have chosen to show many of them alone, thus affording you an opportunity to appreciate the creativity and skilled workmanship used in creating these heirlooms.

Considerable time and thought were expended on every quilt discussed in this book. We tried to photograph each one in an environment appropriate to its age or design. Joyce Horne and Cheryl Schonewille assisted me at all photo sessions. Together we selectively displayed hundreds of quilts in numerous locations. Joyce and Cheryl worked very closely with me on every photograph and also spent considerable time organizing our strategies for capturing the correct mood for each quilt in its unique setting. This involved many hours of planning and researching both the quilts and the layout sites so that we have provided the reader with a glimpse into Ontario's past.

Mary Ann Hull assisted with

the voluminous clerical work. My husband travelled with me while I was recording and cataloguing. I was fortunate to have such a dedicated helpmate to help carry ladders and assist in all the set-ups, as well as doing all the photography for my personal records.

The owners of the quilts have been recognized on pages 158 and 159. It is these people, many of whom are quilters, who are most interested in seeing that Ontario's quilting heritage is recorded before it is lost to the devastating effects of time and wear.

I am very grateful to the following guilds and/or groups: Erie Shores Quilters' Guild, Kawartha Quiltmakers' Guild, Niagara Heritage Quilters' Guild, Ottawa Valley Quilters' Guild, Simcoe County Quilters' Guild, Sudbury and District Quilt and Stitchery Guild, York Heritage Quilters' Guild, Anna Larocque and friends in Sarnia, Janet Rice-Bredin and friends in Thunder Bay, and Lorraine Davidson and friends in Kapuskasing.

Environment Canada Parks Service permitted us to photograph at Fort George and to use their facilities as we required; as did the Niagara Peninsula Conservation Authority, who gave us full use of the Ball Farm, including the interior of the buildings. These two facilities, with all their authentic artifacts, made the photography part of our job much easier, and I am very grateful to the aforementioned agencies for their generosity.

The owners of the Kiely House Heritage Inn c. 1830 in Niagara-on-the-Lake also allowed us to take many photographs in their restored bedrooms and grounds. Countless people juggled their

Mosaic c. 1872, Fletcher, Vermont, Mrs. Charles Webster; **Bear's Paw** c. 1880, Peterborough County, Ontario, Margaret Fitzgerald Mackey

schedules to accommodate us, and to all those interested, co-operative individuals, I wish to express my gratitude.

Many other people shared their time and knowledge, and while they are too numerous to mention by name, they will always be fondly remembered. It was this genuine interest shared by so many that made all the work seem worthwhile.

We are certainly living in a technological era, as the information in this manuscript has been compiled with the aid of a computer. I was assisted by a computer programmer who wrote my program for storing information on each quilt catalogued. I studied more than 2,000 quilts, from which I made my selections for this book. This information is readily retrievable and can be

quickly sorted by design, age, etc., something which heretofore would have taken incalculable hours. With this new technology, collections can be recorded easily and be preserved for future generations to study and enjoy.

I have included instructions for constructing three of the unique quilts found within these pages, and I hope that these will be a catalyst for those readers who

wish to pursue the art of creating heirlooms for future generations to enjoy and admire.

Ontario has a wealth of beautiful old quilts owned by many kind, sharing individuals, and it is to these people that I dedicate this book.

Crazy Ann c. 1890
Proton, Ontario
Elizabeth Mulhall

INTRODUCTION

Quilts have played an interesting role in our history. They have cycled in and out of vogue as technology and economics have changed. In the pre-industrial agricultural world which prevailed during much of the nineteenth century, young girls learned their sewing and quilting skills at home when all homes had quilts to stave off the cold drafts of winter. The pioneer farm home was a domestic manufactory where all family members participated in the economic enterprise of supporting the family unit. It was the women who produced the cloth, clothing, table and bed linens as well as the food products, soaps and candles. During this era, children learned skills at home that would prepare them for their adult roles in society. Sewing, an essential skill, was taught to children as young as two or three, as soon as their fingers could grip a needle.

Following the U.S. Civil War, needlework underwent significant changes, many of which can be attributed to technological advances. Chemical discoveries led to new synthetic dyes which gave the quilter a new colour palette. Changes in retail marketing and mail order brought goods to a wider public. The invention of the sewing machine in 1848 made sewing and piecing much quicker. This new gadget was generally placed in the parlour, where the women would sew in the midst of their families. As Ontario became more industrialized, women began to move out of the home and into the factories.

Quilts became less fashionable in urban homes as woven coverlets gained in popularity. However, quilting was kept alive in the cities thanks to church and missionary groups. The quilting bee was, and still is, a social occasion where people could get together to visit while working creatively. The bee also provided an opportunity to show one's latest creation, exchange new ideas for patchwork, and share news and stories while working on a communal quilt. Quilting bees included all levels of society and were very useful for the skilled needlewoman who wanted an active social life.

Over the years, quilts have formed a "chain of love" linking one generation to another. They have become bonds that join families together more strongly than any legal document.

PIECED QUILTS

A Pieced quilt is one in which the top has been created from separate elements seamed together. The pieces or patches used in these quilts are simple geometric shapes such as squares, triangles, diamonds, rectangles, hexagons and circles. The patches must be cut accurately in order for the pieces to fit together. However, this did not always happen with the utilitarian quilt. The elements were assembled into units called blocks; the blocks were sewn together into strips; the strips were joined to form the completed top. Sometimes a border or borders would be added. The first immigrants were unprepared for the severe Canadian winters and were forced to piece hastily whatever fabric or fabric scraps they had available; aesthetics were not even considered. Some of the pioneers in Québec soon learned from the native people the art of piecing animal skins, and for a time this technique was practised in the early settlements.

Many of Ontario's early settlers came from England, where the Pieced quilt had been popular at the beginning of the eighteenth century, thus they arrived with cutting and piecing experience. However, early in the eighteenth century the government of England had banned the importing of chintzes from India. The needlewomen of the era became very skilled at using every available scrap of chintz in their patchwork. They would salvage chintz from garments, household furnishings or even purchase it on the black market! By 1774 the Crown lifted the ban, printing on cotton resumed, and the English were quick to copy designs from

the East Indian chintzes.

The earliest surviving example of an elaborately pieced English quilt is known as the Levens Hall Patchwork Quilt. It is in England's Victoria and Albert Museum. By the latter half of the eighteenth century more patchwork and appliqué started to appear in England. Most of this early work had a central motif which was bordered. An excellent example of a Medallion quilt executed in Ontario is the one on page 114. It was pieced in about 1827. Great care was taken with the central design, and the borders were often made of variations of geometric patchwork.

The early colonists in Ontario had few resources with which to work. Their quilts incorporated bits of garments and other household textiles and were actually a record of family history. Conditions improved and prosperity brought the availability of new fabrics. Fancy quilts gradually began to appear as part of the parlour decor, and guests had special quilts saved for their arrival. The master bedroom often had the luxury of a special quilt that might have been part of a trousseau or a wedding gift.

Squares and triangles were simple shapes that the nineteenth-century quilter had little trouble sewing. This scrap Crazy Ann quilt was created as a three-colour quilt. The light print has faded considerably and one of the sprigged muslins appears to be quite brown, but it was probably dark blue and has faded with laundering and exposure to light.

While all of these triangles were cut individually, this quilt could be made in a weekend by using quick piecing techniques.

*Detail of **Crazy Ann***

The Mulhall family immigrated to Ontario from County Wicklow, Ireland, in the 1850s, following the Great Potato Famine. John, Elizabeth and their two sons settled in a small farming community north of Guelph, and many of their direct descendants still live in the area. As their family grew in number so did the need for quilts and bedding. It is likely that the Mulhall women quilted together both to increase their productivity and to socialize.

The quilting is a very simple clamshell and fairly widely spaced. Elizabeth was anxious to finish this quilt so that she could make another. Her family grew

steadily until she had a total of nine children. It is highly unlikely that during her lifetime she ever made a quilt from anything other than scraps left over from household sewing. Fortunately, Elizabeth had a sewing machine, which allowed her to machine-piece her quilts. Elizabeth had a good sense of composition, as she very skilfully placed the red units so that the eye must move around the surface.

Old diaries tell us that life in rural Ontario was arduous and often lonely. Marauding animals were described as a common occurrence. Hungry bears roamed the settled areas, scrounging for whatever food scraps were available. In so doing, they left their tracks in the moist ground, and hence many quilt patterns were named for such observations. It is interesting to note when studying pattern names that many of the names directly relate to nature and the settlers' daily surroundings.

Margaret Fitzgerald Mackey made this quilt in the mid-1880s for her granddaughter Jean. Here we see a typical mid-1800s log cabin and buckboard at the Ball farm in Jordan. The cabins were drafty in winter, and this heavy, warm woollen quilt would certainly have been on the bed, warming those beneath it. The back is homespun in 27-inch widths, and it is possible that it was woven from the wool of sheep raised on the family farm in eastern Ontario. Sheep farming was common in that area.

Margaret used the fabrics she had available, and as there was insufficient blue for the sashing and border, some areas have brown sections. It would appear that the sashing and border are also homespun and the remainder is made from suitings. The quilt has been well used and cared for, with carefully mended areas. Margaret was a skilled needlewoman; she was able to quilt the bulky quilt with a simple curved design that was centred in the sashing between two blocks.

Bear's Paw *c. 1880*
Peterborough County, Ontario
Margaret Fitzgerald Mackey

*Detail of **Bear's Paw***

The Parrs were early settlers in the Tintern area of the Niagara Peninsula, having moved there in 1841. Rebecca Parr would have purchased this piece of chintz, printed to resemble a Pieced quilt, in St. Catharines, Ontario. Upon careful inspection, it can be seen that the quilting is sparse and has been randomly done across the surface, with no regard for the mock piecing. Interestingly, this quilt was a special quilt and has never been laundered, even though it has been enjoyed by several generations of Parrs. When Rebecca made her will in 1899 she stated that this quilt was to go to her grandson, Herman.

Cheater Cloth c. 1870, Tintern, Ontario, Rebecca Parr

Quilters are very resourceful when it comes to tricking the eye. This design is sometimes referred to as Snowball and is entirely pieced using straight lines. The circular illusion is accentuated by piecing in each corner a triangle half the size of one of the nine patch squares and quilting these hexagonal shapes with a circular feathered wreath motif. Two-colour quilts were popular in the last quarter of the nineteenth century. This one was executed using a collection of red-and-white prints.

Little is known about the quilter except that she never married, and that she lived in Florida and made quilts for friends and relatives. When she died she left a legacy of 30-plus tops waiting to be quilted. The owner had this top—which has never been laundered—backed and quilted using motifs common to its era.

Snowball *c. 1874*
Florida, quilter unknown

Detail of **Snowball** *showing 2-block construction*

Diamond-in-a-Square *c. 1900, probably made in central Ontario*

Winters are cold in Ontario, and warm quilts were an absolute necessity in order to survive. This Amish-inspired woollen Diamond-in-a-Square was constructed using a dark blanket fabric. Like many woollen quilts, it is very heavy but also exceedingly warm. This quilt has woollen batting and, because of the bulk, has a minimal amount of quilting, which serves only to hold the three layers of fabric together.

Ontario's cold winters and drafty log cabins made it imperative that our early settlers have warm quilts such as the one seen here. When central heat became common, these weighty quilts were no longer required, so they were stored for emergency use. Fortunately, many of them have survived the ravages of time and vermin.

Woollen quilts were an integral part of the bedding inventory of a well-furnished home. A woollen quilt was very much cherished during the long, cold winter months. Here we have two red-and-black quilts which were either saved for guests or used by the parents. Guests were a common occurrence, since travel was slow and often hazardous on the narrow roads of the time. When guests arrived they were always made to feel a part of the household during their visit, which frequently lasted at least a week or longer.

On the upper left we see a traditional Jacob's Ladder variation which has been carefully cut and pieced using a woollen blanket that had become too worn for continued use. A pattern for this appears on page 152. Fabric was scarce, and so by cutting out the less worn areas and using small squares, the quilter could get maximum use from her fabric. Note how the intersections are all pieced blocks—one can only assume there were no pieces large enough to do these squares as one piece. This quilt was made in Blackwater, Ontario, by a Mrs. Ferguson as a gift for her good friend Mary Millward Smith sometime in the late nineteenth century. However, it does appear that the fabric is considerably older than this.

The origin of the quilt on the lower right is unknown, but it has been created from black-and-navy suitings and red worsted tartan wool. The quilter ran out of the red tartan in a section of the border and had to use some red print, which adds to the character of this very warm, heavy quilt.

Neither of these quilts has any batting and they are sparsely quilted with large stitches, as it is impossible to do any fine quilting through such heavy material. These quilts are exceedingly heavy

due to the fabrics used. They would have been taken out of circulation as soon as the homes became warm enough to allow the use of lighter quilts. When central heat became available, they were banished to a cedar chest, to be found by family heirs many years later.

Jacob's Ladder c. 1880
Blackwater, Ontario
Mrs. Ferguson
Hole-in-the-Barn-Door c. 1900
probably made in central Ontario

Sarah Sproule enjoyed hand-piecing. It was something that could be done at leisure in the evening or when sitting and visiting during the winter. Where did quilters get their inspiration for a particular set? Observe the fencing in this farmyard. It displays a square grid motif with a jagged barbed-wire top. Take it and turn it on a point and we see the "set" for this quilt. Barbed wire was used to contain farm animals, and here we see the same effect created with the jagged border, which serves to contain the central motif. Notice the corner treatment of the squares in diagonally opposite corners. They are identical. This gives an axial effect to the design. As was common, the quilting in the central white and red areas is quite extensive and is a vine-and-leaf motif, while the outer area has been simply cross-hatched. The outer areas of the quilt would fall over the sides of the bed and therefore the quilting did not need to be as detailed.

Solomn's Temple c. 1890
Cannington, Ontario
Sarah Sproule

Sawtooth Diamond c. 1910
Lanark County, Ontario
Ellen Fair

In the early twentieth century most unmarried women had no profession. Rather they would live with a friend or relative and share in the household chores. Ellen Fair was such a woman. She usually lived with her brother George in Lanark County, but she would travel from relative to relative, spending time with each, and while visiting she would sew and also make quilts for the family.

This Sawtooth variation is a wonderful example of linsey-woolsey. Probably while visiting some relative, Ellen helped to card, spin and weave the wool which was so necessary for bedding and clothing during the long, cold winters in eastern Ontario.

This quilt has been machine-pieced. While it would have taken hundreds of hours to cut and piece all the triangles used in this design, it allowed the quilter an opportunity to use up many small scraps of fabric while creating a favourite design. The quilt is heavy and cumbersome, so it was sparsely quilted with a clamshell design using black thread. The quilting was very difficult due to the weight of the fabric, compounded by the bulk of the batting. It is quite likely that the wool for this batting came from the family farm, as most farms in eastern Ontario had sheep.

Cleaning quilts was time-consuming and arduous, so black was a favourite colour for winter quilts. It did not show soil and hence would be cleaned less frequently than lighter-coloured cotton summer quilts. However, these quilts would have been well aired and beaten before being stored for the summer. Many stored quilts are damaged by moths, but present cleaning methods make it easier to care for these treasured family heirlooms.

It is interesting to observe that the quilt on page 15 has the identical set, only the corner elements have been handled differently and they have different border treatments.

Sawtooth Variation *c. 1870*
Québec

Two-colour quilts have long been a favourite of quilters. The red fabric is known as "turkey red," which is an intense red and very colourfast. Little is known about this quilt which was purchased in Québec. It has been entirely hand-pieced by a skilled and innovative needlewoman; all the triangles in the borders have been perfectly matched to create the necessary sharp points required for the design.

It is possible that the quilter used a saw blade or a gear wheel as her inspiration for the central medallion. It has been applied with an overcast stitch and was probably designed by "paper-cutting" techniques in which she took a piece of paper, folded it in eighths, and then cut her shape, which created this blade when the paper was opened out. It is also possible that she actually traced around a saw blade directly onto the fabric. It is interesting to note the corner treatment. Quilters did not worry about making their corners uniform. These quilts were made for beds, and when lying on a bed you cannot see the four corners at one time, so a flaw is not apparent.

This quilter enjoyed quilting, as the surface of the quilt has been extensively worked. All the triangles have been outline-quilted, and the four central triangles have also been quilted in rows one-half inch apart following the triangle shape. The remainder of the surface has been crosshatched with a grid of less than one-half inch.

As these cotton quilts were laundered over the years, the fabric and batting have shrunk, giving the quilt surface a slightly puckered look, which is what gives the surface a dimension that is enjoyed by quilt enthusiasts. This quilt has received excellent care by its owners, and its appearance has only been enhanced by its many careful launderings.

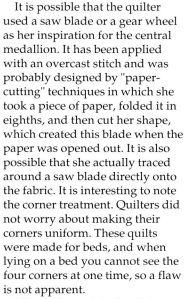

*Detail of **Sawtooth Variation***

Florence Bunker chose to make this Broken Stairway design using a brown sprigged-muslin fabric and her sewing machine for much of the piecing. However, she hand-stitched all the large blocks with brown print and muslin triangles, as she probably had difficulty with the bias edges when piecing on her sewing machine. The sprigged muslin has a serpentine stripe within its design, and this allowed Florence to machine-stitch the binding on the top side of the quilt, as well as stitch around all of the small brown blocks. Just as a set of stairs is built to withstand constant usage, so Florence constructed her quilt to withstand the rigours of daily use in an active household of adults and children.

The very popular clamshell motif has been used for the quilting design and it softens the sharpness of the central motif while accentuating the illusion of a broken stairway. Here we see the quilt photographed at Queenston Heights with a very long stairway in the background. This stairway, like that in the quilt, is interrupted before reaching Brock's Monument, a favourite historic attraction in Queenston. Brock's Monument was erected in 1824 and some 16 years later was blown up by a vagabond named Lett. It was rebuilt in 1856 and majestically dominated the horizon for the next 85 years, until Brock's outstretched arm came crashing to the ground during a heavy gale. Fortunately, it was repaired and continues to welcome visitors from far and wide.

Like Brock's Monument, this quilt exhibits evidence of the effects of age and use, but it exudes the feeling "Yes, I have been enjoyed!"

Broken Stairway *c. 1930*
Markham, Ontario
Florence Bunker

A historic treasure, this top has been well cared for and never laundered. It was pieced by Mary Dickerson Winn, 1825-1910, who lived in Fairfax, Stanstead County, Québec. Mary married Jacob Winn in 1842 and family history records that she had three daughters, ages two, three and seven, at the time she made this top. It is a marvel to imagine that a woman with a young family could have had the time to cut and piece the hundreds of triangles which are used in this top. Jacob Winn died of yellow fever in 1857 while on his way to California, leaving Mary a young widow. In 1867 Mary married Sherburn Locke and was affectionately known as Grandma Locke to the residents of her community, for whom she made many quilts in addition to those made for her family members.

Why Mary never quilted this top will forever remain a mystery. However, it has been photographed with a section of the back showing so that you can examine how precisely every piece has been fitted together and sewn with minute stitches. The Shelburne Museum in Shelburne, Vermont, has a quilt of this identical pattern and set, which dates from about 1776 and was extremely popular for many years. This is a very complex pattern to piece together, as the "fans" must be pieced first, followed by the dividing borders, which are pieced in strips. Larger blocks are formed by completing the fan blocks and then seaming four of the blocks together and sashing them with the border strip, which has a pieced Sunburst block carefully set in at every intersection. It is a remarkable example of cutting, piecing and sewing, considering that quilters of the era did not generally have access to rulers or compasses. It is quite likely that Mary was given the pattern and was careful with her cutting and

piecing, thus the top went together with no unforeseen problems. Indeed, it is fortunate that this top was never completed, as we have the opportunity to study the sewing and cutting techniques of the early settlers.

New York Beauty c. 1850
Stanstead County, Québec
Mary Dickerson Winn

Detail of **New York Beauty**

Homespun c. 1880, Montréal, Québec, Maria (Bice) Graham

Maria (Bice) Graham came to Canada with her parents, United Empire Loyalists who settled near Montréal. In 1831 she married Colonel John Graham and moved to Ops Township, Victoria County, Ontario. Maria became a renowned weaver, and clients travelled from miles around and visited while she wove their woollen yarn.

This quilt was originally made from material woven by Maria. Eventually it became badly worn on the edges, so her granddaughter—true to the saying "necessity is the mother of invention"—used the tops of worn men's socks to make a colourful border, then rebound the quilt with some of the bright homespun backing. The early settlers were frugal out of necessity; they would use and reuse unworn areas in articles of clothing, recycling every square inch.

Here we see an excellent assortment of weaves and colours popular in rural Ontario in the late nineteenth century. This quilt was meant to be a winter quilt and has woollen batting for additional warmth. While it is a very thick quilt, wool is relatively easy to needle and Maria did some simple quilting in order to hold the layers of fabric together.

This quilt was photographed, complete with bed and straw mattress, in an early Ontario log cabin. Such log cabins were small and furnishings were quite spartan.

Nothing is known about this Scrap quilt which was made during the reign of Queen Victoria. It is interesting to observe that there is one triangle which has been cut very carefully to preserve as much of Queen Victoria as possible.

While the interiors of many farm homes were very drab, colourful fabrics were available. By 1900 fabric was becoming easier to obtain and prints were becoming more colourful. In order to brighten the log cabin's interior, the housewife would choose bright prints such as the one shown on the back of this quilt, which is a close colour match to the paint on the table. A farm woman would probably also have had some bright house-dresses for the afternoon or for when she was doing lighter chores, and these would have brought a cheery feeling both to the wearer and to those around her. Notice that even the scrap used on the crock lid is the same bright red so prevalent at this time.

1,000 Pyramids c. 1900
origin unknown

Colour was very important in the farm home. Bedrooms were generally quite dull and it was the women's role to embellish the rooms with their needle skills. Red, yellow and green were popular colours during the mid to late 1800s.

The Triple Irish Chain was made by Elizabeth Quantz, who was one of the earliest settlers in Markham Township along with her husband, Frederick, and his family. Frederick was born in England and his father, Melchior, served with the British army in North America during the American War of Independence. After he was mustered out of the army, Melchior returned to England to join a group of emigrés led by William Berczy from Germany. This group of six families arrived first in New York State, where they worked as sharecroppers for a short period of time. In the late 1700s Berczy heard of free land in Upper Canada. The six families, along with Berczy, came to Markham Township, where they home-steaded. Frederick and Elizabeth lived a long and happy life in Ontario and had 16 children. Elizabeth made this quilt without the aid of glasses when she was over 90 years of age. She certainly would have had a large assort-ment of scraps from which to choose fabrics for her quilts. The "lightning" border is somewhat unusual, as it is quite distracting when viewing the central design. However, like all quilters, Elizabeth apparently wanted to try something new, even at age 90! This quilt, along with several others, is now cherished by her great-great-granddaughter, Elma.

The Nine-patch quilt was made by Frances Williams from leftover dress scraps. It was intended to be used, and certainly it has been enjoyed by many family members and relatives. It presently has a place of honour in the home of Fanny's great-niece.

Madame's Maple Leaves is a rare example of French-Canadian quilting. It has 36 stylized maple leaves which are arranged on the diagonal and appliquéd with an almost invisible stitch. This design can be referred to as Québécois, as the style was taught in Québec 100 years ago in convent schools where young ladies learned the art of "fine, even stitching." The quilter gave this quilt a patriotic flair by appliquéing maple leaves between the central leaf motifs. The batting is very thin, which seems common to many French-Canadian quilts, so they do not have much loft to them. Since the batting disintegrates with age, we see here an example of a perfectly executed design and stitching.

The Pieced Peony appliqué of American origin was probably made as a wedding gift. However, the quilter used fabrics that were vegetable dyed, and most of these fabric dyes were unstable and have faded. This quilt has the traditional crosshatch stitching that was used extensively during the nineteenth century and much of the twentieth century. Many small stitches and close quilting add to the charm of these quilts that are so enjoyed by quilt lovers.

Quilts were frequently stored on display racks such as we see here. Cupboards were nonexistent in early homes, so racks were found in halls or bedrooms, wherever space permitted. Bedrooms were painted neutral colours and decorating remained simple, thus it was the quilts that added colour and warmth to the spartan rooms. By changing the colour scheme of the quilts hanging on a rack or covering the bed, one could easily change the appearance of a room while still keeping the necessities of life close at hand.

Triple Irish Chain c. 1870
Markham Township, Ontario
Elizabeth Quantz
Madame's Maple Leaves c. 1875
Québec
Nine-patch c. 1870,
Glen Williams, Ontario
Frances William
Pieced Peony c. 1880
United States

Indian Cross and Star c. 1900
origin unknown

Handpiecing was easy to do and relaxing in the evening after an active day of household activities. Many summer quilts were created using pastel-coloured scraps from the fabric scrap bag, and the finished quilts created an impression of colourful spring gardens. Gardens were very important to farm women. They enjoyed the assorted colours found in a carefully planned flower or vegetable garden, a welcome relief after the long, drab winter months.

Quilters would often trade fabric scraps in order to increase the variety of fabrics they had available to use in any given quilt. While this is a Scrap quilt, the quilter's supply must have been limited, as it is easy to see that the same fabrics have been used in several blocks. It can only be assumed that the quilter lived in a remote area or didn't have time to participate in a local quilting bee.

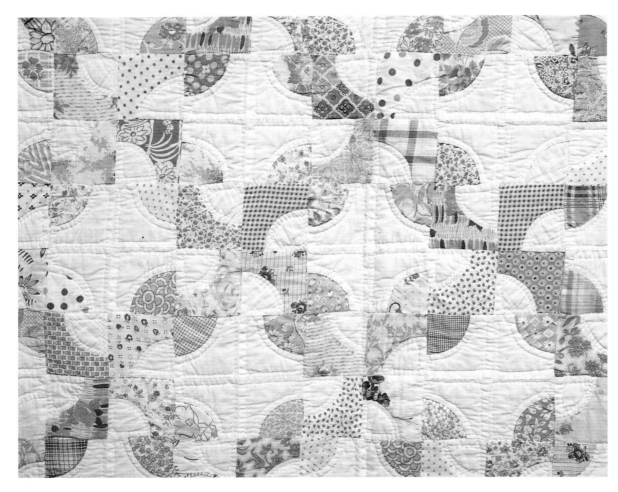

Scrap quilts were very popular during the 1930s, as women were still doing much of the family sewing and economic times were extremely difficult for many people. The scraps from children's clothes, pyjamas and housedresses kept scrap bags full and were a wonderful source of colourful fabrics. These quilts enable the present viewer to study the types of fabrics available to sewers in various areas of the country at this time.

Miss Philpot took great pride in her piecing. Her squares are all of identical size and all her corners match perfectly. This was not easy, as sharp pencils and rulers were not always available to quilters. She probably spent many hours a day sewing, as this quilt has 832 2-inch squares. All of the squares have a bias seam that requires special care when sewing, to prevent distortion and to ensure that the quilt lies flat when completed. She also arranged her scraps along the border so that where the design elements meet at the outside edge, the scraps are the same, thus creating scallops along the edge of the quilt for added interest.

This top was purchased by a quilter from Hanmer, Ontario, and was bordered and quilted by her. She now proudly displays it on a guest bed for all to enjoy.

Drunkard's Path c. 1930, Woodstock, Ontario, Miss Philpot

SUMMER/WINTER

Log Cabin, Straight Furrows *c. 1950, Sarnia, Ontario,*
Railroad Variation *c. 1880, Leamington, Ontario, Catherine Evans*

Detail of **Railroad Variation** *showing piecing of two blocks*

The Ball house was built in 1840 and contains the furniture and artifacts that belonged to the Ball families who lived in the home until it was given to the Niagara Peninsula Conservation Authority in the mid-1960s. In the master bedroom we see a handpieced 1880 Railroad Variation scrap quilt. Catherine Evans pieced over 3,000 1-inch triangles from her scrap bag to construct this top.

The mustard yellow, as it was often called, has been carefully pieced. You will notice that the intersections within each block contain six triangles.

This special quilt was always on Catherine's bed during her lifetime and remained on the bed for another generation, as her daughter lived in the family home after the death of her parents. This quilt has been much loved and enjoyed for over 100 years. Considering it was made by lamplight and that every triangle was carefully cut, one cannot begin to imagine how many hundreds of hours would have gone into its piecing. Great care was also taken with the quilting, as three different quilting designs were used: clamshell along the border, cables in the sashing, and throughout the top there are some straight lines in the middle of the blocks. Not only was Catherine an accomplished piecer, she was also very skilled at quilting. Her quilting stitches are so small as to be the envy of any aspiring quilter.

On the chair we see a summer quilt of a much later period (c. 1950s). Log Cabin quilts have been a perennial favourite. It was an effective design for using up a large number of scraps. Without too much difficulty, scraps could be sorted into lights and darks and assembled into blocks, using the scraps just as they came off the scrap pile.

Quilts have not always been treasured by those who have received them. As urban areas grew and machine-made linens became easy to procure, many housewives cast aside tradition and purchased woollen blankets and bedspreads. This quilt met the fate of many and ended up in a garage sale, where it was purchased for the paltry sum of $10. The new owner, Margaret, took it home and carefully laundered it, which brought to life the vivid colours in this wonderful assortment of fabrics from the 1950s.

It is interesting to note how the appearance of a room can be transformed by changing the quilt on the bed and adding or subtracting a few appointments, such as a vase of flowers. On page 26, we see the same bedroom as it might have looked during the fall and winter with its sombre-coloured quilts and only a few flowers for colour. It is certainly refreshing to see a lighter-coloured quilt used during the warmer seasons.

As the weather became cooler, the farm wife would put a warmer quilt on the bed. Here at the Ball home, we see a very warm fan quilt constructed from men's suiting, some heavy cottons and a little velvet, all very carefully arranged in a swirling fan design. For the background, Irene (Lucas) Roberts used a black worsted wool and a dark green wool, and carefully intermingled the green and black blocks.

Irene certainly intended this to be a good quilt, as she

embroidered her name in the block at the lower right edge and feather-stitched all the fan sections for added interest. Irene also quilted each block with an arc, which softens the linear appearance of the fans.

The Straight Furrows Log Cabin is hanging on the screen, should it be required for extra warmth. This quilt was made from taffetas and silks, many of which are rotting and exposing the muslin foundation. Doris Parr enjoyed cutting and piecing Log Cabin blocks, as

this Straight Furrows quilt has been constructed from a 3-inch block. In order to hold the top to the batting and back, Doris has used orange thread and tied the layers to the back.

Granny's Fan c. 1917
Brooke Township, Ontario
Irene (Lucas) Roberts
Log Cabin, Straight Furrows c. 1850
McGregor, Ontario
Doris Parr

Log Cabin, Sunshine and Shadow c. 1910, Utopia, Ontario, a Bell woman

Spools c. 1920, Woodstock, Ontario, Mrs. Soper
Dresden Plate c. 1940, Alliston, Ontario

The young lady who slept in this well-appointed room at the Ball home in Jordan, Ontario, was very fortunate to have a treadle sewing machine. In those days a young woman approaching matrimonial age would have spent many spare hours preparing for the future. She was expected to enter into marriage with a complete set of household linens, including a number of quilts.

We see the room as it might have appeared in the seasonal transition from fall to winter and spring to summer from the 1920s to 1940s. Women took great pride in their work, but they had few opportunities to display it, so the bedroom became important as a place for exhibiting their artistic creativity.

The Log Cabin quilt on the bed has been created using suiting fabric for the dark logs, and all the centres and binding have been cut from velvet. The light logs have been cut from heavy shirting fabrics, which kept the weight of the logs uniform. The backing is also very colourful, as it has been cut from drapery fabric known as cretonne cloth. Log Cabin quilts were not always quilted, as they were often too thick; however, with this quilt, one of the Bell women from Utopia, Ontario, managed to quilt between the blocks in order to hold the three layers of fabric together.

On the same bed is a scrap Dresden Plate which was made in the Alliston area. A Scrap quilt is sometimes difficult to date since some of the scraps may be much older than others. Scrap bags were generally passed down from one generation to the next. It is possible this quilt was made by a church group or a young quilter, as the blocks are quite substantial, the quilting very simple, and the stitches reasonably large. However, these quilts are always favourites, as they are very colour-ful, with a wonderful array of fabrics that look charming in any bedroom.

At the sewing machine we see a perfectly pieced Spools quilt. It too is a Scrap quilt, but the scraps used are much more muted than those in the Dresden Plate, and the background is made of bleached sugar bags with some of the markings still visible in a few of the sections. This quilt would have been pieced on a treadle sewing machine such as the one pictured, then simply quilted with straight lines, so as not to interrupt the piecing design.

Mrs. Soper enjoyed her time spent sewing, and she also taught the owner of this quilt, Bea Haley, to sew as a young woman. Mrs. Soper was born in 1835, before the sewing machine was invented. Long before she died in 1935, she had acquired a machine and become very proficient at using it for her piecing and quilting projects. Bea enjoyed visiting with her and learned most of her sewing skills from her very talented friend, who made this quilt and entrusted it to Bea's mother to give to her for her wedding in 1947, many years after Mrs. Soper's death. Thanks to Mrs. Soper, Bea has a wonderful quilt and an excellent foundation of sewing skills.

Here we have a well-used and well-loved winter quilt made from flannelette scraps. The fabric for this sombre quilt probably came from pyjama or shirting flannelette. The maker was probably of French-Canadian extraction, since this quilt was purchased in Catalogue de Chez Nous, West Brome, Québec. She may have had numerous growing sons for whom she sewed new warm pyjamas every winter. The backing is made of bleached feed bags with some of the markings still slightly visible. One bag is marked "Montreal Quaker Mills."

The grey tartan fabric used as sashing and border was probably blue when it was new and has faded with time and laundering. The owner of this quilt has researched the history of its feed bags. They came from mills in the Brome area, some of which closed at the turn of the century. The batting is a heavy cotton, which makes this tied quilt warm and durable.

Album Block *c. 1900*
West Brome, Québec

Farm homes were cold and drafty during the fall and winter seasons, and a worn quilt was often folded and woven through the ladders of a chair so that the occupant could enjoy this added warmth against his or her back. Worn quilts were never discarded, as they could always serve a functional as well as decorative purpose on the furniture in the sitting area.

Nothing is known about this quilt except that it came from Amherstburg, Ontario, which was settled by Black slaves fleeing oppression in the United States. This quilt is from a log cabin in the area and was probably made by a former slave. It has now found a home at the Bittersweet Bed and Breakfast in Kingsville, Ontario, where it is used for display purposes, for guests to enjoy.

Goose Tracks c. 1930, Burk's Falls, Ontario, Caroline and Emma Rousell

Caroline and Emma Rousell were sisters who lived in Burk's Falls at the turn of the century. Like many farm residents of the era, they probably did much of their quilting in the evening after completing their daily chores. This fireplace in the renovated and restored 1830 Kiely House in Niagara-on-the-Lake is in a room now used as a sitting area, but which was originally a cooking area.

Depending on the area of the country in which you reside, this pattern is known as Duck's Foot, Bear's Paw or Goose Tracks. Living in northern Ontario, Caroline and Emma would certainly have been familar with bears, and it is quite likely that in this region it was known as Bear's Paw or Goose Tracks.

The blocks have been randomly arranged with some regard for

balance of colour. Most of the blocks have different scraps, and the batting of this quilt is wool which came from sheep raised on the farm. Many farm homes had cotton quilts with woollen batting, which made them very light and warm. Wool batting is easy to quilt. When properly cared for, as this quilt has been, the batting does not disintegrate or migrate with age and laundering, like cotton batting does.

Quilts were frequently used to cover sofas, as they gave a room a feeling of coziness, and if the fire died down too soon they could be used as a throw. Who knows, the sofa might also have been worn or stained. Whatever the reason, quilts were found draped over the furniture in many well-appointed homes. This quilt has a red print border on one edge only. For interest, this border has been placed along the lower edge of the sofa. There is little quilting on this quilt, so it was probably intended to be used as a throw or on the parents' bed during the winter.

Indian Hatchet c. 1890
Amherstburg, Ontario

Rhoda Lydia (Springsted) Davison made this Scrap quilt utilizing her scraps and augmenting them with some striped fabric remnants which came from the McGregor Shirt Company of Hamilton. Rhoda made a deliberate attempt to arrange the blocks on the diagonal while arranging the colours so they do not jar the eye.

Farm homes were cool late at night when baby needed to be nursed. Here we have the quilt draped over the rocking chair in readiness for the next feeding, whenever it should occur.

Cotton Boll c. 1920
Hamilton, Ontario
Rhoda Lydia (Springsted) Davison

Triple Irish Chain c. 1930, Mount Julia's, Ontario, Mrs. Thompson

The Depression saw everybody making frugal use of their scraps. Prior to the 1930s Irish Chains were generally two-colour quilts, but here Mrs. Thompson organized her assorted scraps in a most pleasing manner—though the quilt was never used. The scraps used here were probably from aprons and housedresses or children's clothing, and some of them are quite thin. However, Mrs. Thompson was a perfectionist, as the squares are perfectly matched.

Upon completion, the top was stored for future use, and it was not until the 1980s that Muriel Wilson of Apsley decided to quilt it using a stylized design in the open areas and "in the ditch" (in the seam line) in the chain blocks.

In the background we see a Crazy quilt draped over the settee. Crazy quilts were generally made for decorative purposes and were seldom used. The fabrics were scrap velvets, suitings, silk or taffeta lining, and they were heavily embellished with embroidery.

The bed-sitting room at the Kiely House in Niagara-on-the-

Lake has some of the early furniture still in it, and it is much the same as it was when the previous owners lived there. The fireplace waits to be lit while the guests linger over a book after a day spent exploring the historic town of Niagara. There is also an inviting pile of quilts on the window bench, should the occupants feel the need of yet another one on their bed.

Two-colour quilts were very much favoured during the latter half of the nineteenth century and the first half of the twentieth century. On the bed we see a variation of Single Irish Chain. This quilt was made by Catherine Bayliss in 1930. Catherine enjoyed using her sewing machine and had mastered the problems of seaming many small units. This variation of Single Irish Chain is also known as Burgoyne Surrounded, and it would indeed seem that Burgoyne had no avenue for escape. The blue for this quilt was probably purchased for this purpose. It appears as if Catherine ran out of fabric, as it is only bordered top and bottom.

Laura Ashenhurst purchased a McCalls pattern for 30 cents in 1935 which gave her instructions for piecing her blue and white Star quilt. At the time, Laura was a teacher at a small county school near the village of Apsley in Peterborough County. She had her father make the required template from galvanized metal so that she would not wear the edge by repeatedly tracing around it. This quilt top is totally pieced by hand. Laura enjoyed her handpiecing and chose to border this quilt with numerous diamonds in two sizes, each of which she cut individually. Laura's pieced border is very complex, while Catherine chose not to include a detailed border on her Irish Chain—time did not always permit the luxury of a border. It was then stored away until 1989, when Laura had the time and inclination to quilt it. This quilt has considerably more loft to it than Catherine's due to the fact that polyester batting was used. It has not been laundered, so we see no dimension being created due to the shrinking process of the top, batting and backing.

Burgoyne Surrounded c. 1930, Wexford, Ontario, Catherine Bayliss
Lone Star Variation 1935, Apsley, Ontario, Laura Ashenhurst

Stencilling has been in and out of vogue but has never enjoyed great popularity. Generally, the paint pigments hardened on the fabric and were not easily washable. Quilts, being bedcoverings, require washing, so quilters did not usually waste their time with this technique.

This attractive quilt was made as a wedding gift for Mary Jane ("Jennie") Butler , who was born in 1858 in Bloomsburg, Ontario. Mary Jane came from a family of quilters and we see her in the photo on the left, along with her quilting clamp, which was probably also a gift, as it has been ornately carved and has been well used. Not only was this quilt a gift, it was used, laundered and enjoyed by Jennie throughout her life. It is apparent that sunlight has faded some areas of the sashing, but the quilt is still in excellent condition and the paint has not yet hardened or damaged the fabric.

This quilt may be known as Forbidden Fruit to the family, but today it could be titled Treasured Fruit.

*Stencilled **Forbidden Fruit** c. 1860 Bloomsburg, Ontario*

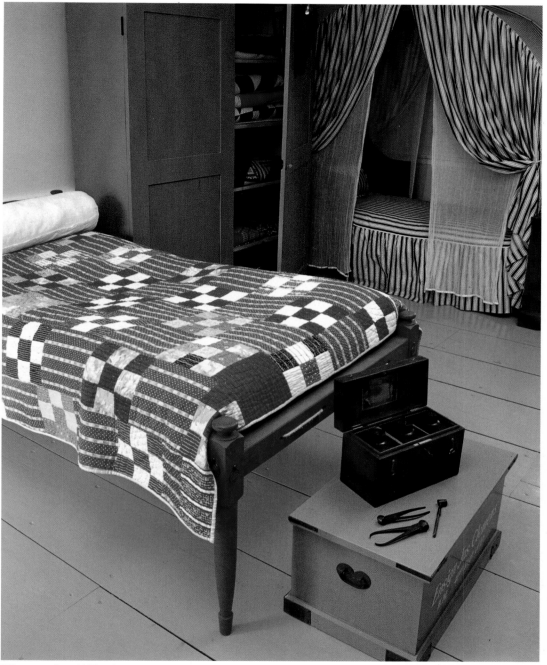

by Lottie L. Mann in about 1910. During her youth, Lottie did not particularly enjoy sewing, rather she preferred to be working on the farm with her husband, Will—milking, haying or tending the family vegetable and flower gardens. Lottie lived a long and productive life; she was born in 1887 and died in 1986. In the later years of her life, when she had more leisure time, she continued with her quilting, and one of her quilts won a prize at the Lakefield Fair.

Rope beds were quite common, and the feather mattress has been turned back to reveal the frame and weaving of the rope. Sitting on the rope is the key which was used to tighten the pegs. This was the origin of the phrase "night, night, sleep tight."

Rope bed showing key to tighten frame

Nine-patch *c. 1910*
Bridgeworth, Ontario
Lottie L. Mann

This warm Nine-patch quilt was photographed on a junior officer's bed at Fort George in Niagara-on-the-Lake. Two officers shared this room. We see the quilt on a Canadian-made rope bed, while the room-mate has a cotton spread and canopy complete with mosquito netting on his English-made "campaign" bed. We also see some quilts and woven coverlets behind the doors of the shared armoire, and it is anybody's guess as to how many of these belonged to each officer.

The scrap Nine-patch was made

Appliqué Thistle c. 1880, Tillsonburg, Ontario, Annie Allin

The quilts on this page were photographed in the senior officer's living area at Fort George in Niagara-on-the-Lake. These quarters are very grandiose by fort standards, as we see his "campaign" chest/desk complete with its appointments in the background.

The Paper Cut quilt has been lifted off the heavily draped canopy bed and displayed over the bright floral reproduction chintz-upholstered chair. Sprigged muslin was very popular for quilting because of its minute design. This thistle design is a well-executed paper-cut appliqué which has been applied to the background block with a tiny overcast stitch. This design was created by folding a piece of paper into quarters and then drawing and cutting the pattern from the folded edge. When the paper was opened, the quilter had a perfectly symmetrical design. Likewise, when she cut her appliqué, the fabric was also folded into quarters and the quarter pattern placed along the fabric fold.

A time-consuming quilt such as this one was probably made for a special event or a bride's trousseau. Since Annie Allin was married in December 1887, it is logical to assume that the quilt predates her wedding. Annie was a prolific quilter and her quilts were made to be used, but they were also well cared for. This quilt was backed with flannelette so that it would not slip off the bed, and it has been quilted using a crosshatch design.

Handpiecing and small bias-edged pieces were not a problem to quilters who enjoyed "hand-work." Anna Weicker pieced and quilted this Tree of Life quilt about 1900. The family feels that it was probably made as a wedding gift. Leisure time was quite limited, but when a quilter chose to make a quilt as a wedding gift she always put forth her best effort. In order to create this gift in a reasonable length of time, it is quite likely that Anna would have taken a small bag of sewing with her when she went visiting, so that she could piece a few of the small green and white squares while socializing with friends or relatives. Anna was very careful with her quilting design. She cross-hatched the sashing and borders, but the blocks which were positioned on the diagonal have only straight lines for the quilting.

Green dyes were not always stable and it is probable that the trees in this quilt were considerably greener when it was created. It was not until after World War I that manufacturers were able to create good colourfast dyes for fabrics.

This quilt was photographed over the senior officer's travelling trunk, which is fairly large. It has a "faux" finish on it and some of the design peeks out along the edge. It would have been necessary for the senior officer to stay at the fort for long periods of time, so he would have provided himself with a well-furnished sleeping and working area. His bed is draped and canopied with a reproduction roller chintz print that has been matched closely to the original in design and colour. He would probably also have had a quilt under the spread on the bed.

Tree of Life or *Pine Tree* c. 1900
East Zorra Township, Ontario, Anna Weicker

Boston Common 1938
Apsley, Ontario
Laura Ashenhurst

Laura Ashenhurst was a teacher in Peterborough County in 1938 when she made this quilt—perhaps a trip around the world was one of her dreams. She enjoyed relaxing and piecing by lamplight in the evenings. Shopping was not easy in rural areas, so Laura bought her fabrics from the Eaton's or Simpsons catalogues, which were delivered free of charge to most households. We can only imagine the feeling of hope, imagination and excitement as Laura selected this wonderful array of prints from her catalogues, then cut and arranged them one at a time into this Boston Common set.

Each block was cut using a 2-inch template which included her seam allowance. When the piecing was completed, Laura put the top away along with its lining, to be completed at a later date. She subsequently married and was eventually widowed. In 1987 she went back to quilting, purchased the batting, and completed this colourful quilt during the long, lonely winter months. Since quilting was enjoying a revival, coloured quilting thread was readily available, so Laura chose to do her quilting with purple quilting thread.

Scrap quilts are a perfect way to empty a scrap bag. Olla Martens took care in organizing her scraps so that she created many design units. Each unit starts with a simple Nine-patch block. The overall block is built up so that it appears as a Square-on-the-Point block, and each unit has a common white border unit to define it. Olla had sufficient green print as well as the light print to sash each unit, and it is this sashing print which serves to highlight each postage-stamp block.

While this appears to be a simple quilt, considerable time was spent in organizing scraps and placing the design units so that they would have a pleasing top when all the units were assembled and sashed. The quilting is quite simple—straight lines which do not detract from the piecing design but which serve to add highlights and hold the layers together.

This quilt has been given excellent care and is still in mint condition, serving as a wonderful legacy to Olla's design skills and workmanship. It is now being used and enjoyed by her granddaughter.

Philadelphia Pavement c. 1940, Bellevue, Michigan, Olla Martens

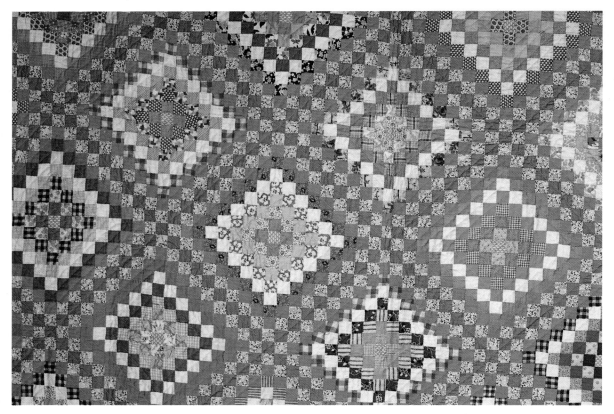

Block detail of
Philadelphia Pavement

Tail of Benjamin's Kite c. 1890
Cleveland, Ohio
Claire Merrick

This Tail of Benjamin's Kite Scrap quilt was made by Claire Merrick, and it has been all handpieced. Claire was careful to use her scraps in blocks of colour. However, upon careful examination it can be seen that she ran out of some of the prints and that she skilfully selected a section of a blending print and seamed her print blocks where necessary.

The Merricks eventually moved to eastern Ontario from Ohio. Many rural farm homes had children's beds tucked into the dormers created by sloping roofs. Ceilings were lower in the back rooms on the second level of farm homes, as this made it easier to heat the upstairs in the winter. This colourful Scrap quilt has been simply quilted with diagonal lines which accent the diagonal set of the pattern. The creative housewife could add a touch of colour to a loft corner by her careful choice of fabrics.

The Double-X quilt is also a Scrap quilt, which has been carefully pieced by machine and kept in a trunk for many years. It was given to its present owner, who added the red border and proceeded to back and quilt it. It now makes a colourful statement on this antique pine bed.

Double-X
origin unknown

Nine-patch Variation c. 1880, Campden, Ontario, Araminta Jane (Moyer) Parr

Araminta Jane Moyer lived in Campden, and these two quilts were made before she married Daniel Wesley Parr in 1893. She was a schoolteacher up until her marriage, when by law she was required to retire. It was not until after 1938 that married women were allowed to be employed as teachers. Since Araminta worked in St. Catharines, it is likely that the fabrics for these quilts were purchased at either McLaren's or Tait's fabric stores, which were opposite each other in the downtown shopping area.

Shades of brown fabric were popular in the Niagara Peninsula during this period (the quilt on page 61 has a similar fabric used for the background). The backing fabric for the quilt on the arm of the chesterfield is the same as the backing for the quilt on page 61.

The Parrs were early settlers in the Tintern area, arriving in 1841. They purchased their farm property, and it was occupied and farmed by succeeding generations until 1972, when it was sold. Quilts were always used in the Parr home, and the two shown here represent part of the family collection. Quilts were sufficiently important in many homes, including the Parrs', that they were mentioned in family wills. These two quilts were left to two different sons in Araminta's will.

In the basket we see a copy of *Godey's Lady's Book* dated 1855. The magazine was published in Philadelphia and came out every month. In it there are patterns for clothes, as well as embroidery patterns, quilting techniques and snippets of advice on matters related to daily living. It was a popular publication during the latter half of the nineteenth century.

The Meiji Gate 1991
Windsor, Ontario
Betty Ives

Jet travel has made moving around the world much easier. Betty Ives attended a quilt exposition in Tokyo in 1990, and at that time collected some Oriental fabrics, together with many memories. Laser-cut tools have been available to the serious quilter for a few years, so accurate cutting and piecing is now possible and in fact expected for any competition piece.

Historically, quilts were created to record significant family events. Betty chose to record her memories of what she saw on a particular day in Tokyo.

Tokyo is a city teeming with people hustling and bustling, jostling each other. It is noisy— horns blowing, brakes squealing, people talking. And in the middle of all of this is the Meiji Shrine. This quilt depicts what Betty saw as she passed through the gates into the long, tree-lined lane which led away from the hurly-burly of the street noise and congestion into this realm of peace and quiet.

Here we see the gates, which were a dark red. The red piecing is an artistic interpretation of Japanese houses—crowded, with many angles, colours and shapes. She has used crazy piecing to create these houses. The lattice-work depicts the light as it shines through the gate at a given moment, and at the top we see her interpretation of the mountains and sky.

This quilt is an excellent example of the new direction in quilting taken by those artistic piecers who wish to design and make quilts for purposes other than bedding.

Evening Star c. 1930, Québec

The owner purchased this quilt at an antique store in Montréal and knows nothing of its history. However, like all quilts of the 1930s, it was made to be used, as it is both machine-pieced and quilted with very thin batting. The design elements are first quilted "in the ditch" (in the seam line) then the star effect is expanded by continuous quilting lines through the centre seam of the design elements.

Fabrics of the 1930s were very colourful and could be randomly pieced into small design elements since the scale of the prints was reasonably small. Picnics were a popular Sunday activity during the pleasant summer months, and this bright, functional quilt adds to the festive mood of a picnic on a pleasant sunny day with friends and family.

While this is a Scrap quilt, it has five angled strips that make up a block. In order for the design to meet when the blocks are seamed together, all the strips must be accurately cut and seamed. Annie Allin was an accomplished quilter; her piecing is perfect and her calibre of quilting is what all quilters strive to achieve. Not only was the piecing of the design difficult, an assortment of quilting techniques were used to enhance the various areas. Her choice of border design and fabric give this Scrap quilt a picture-frame appearance.

Endless Chain c. 1880
Durham, Ontario
Annie Allin

Homes have only so many beds, thus prolific quilters tired of making bed quilts turned their energies to "art" quilts for the wall. Jackie Black has taken a modernistic approach to the traditional equilateral triangle, the shape used to create this stunning piece of artistry. Interfacing was fused to the lamé fabrics before they were cut, in order to reduce the amount of fraying. Strip-piecing techniques were used in the construction of the gears, which depict a fantasy world of mechanization in the night sky while accounting for the regularity of the daylight and evening hours. Jackie chose a black satin coat-lining fabric for her background to complete this dramatic dimensional wall hanging.

Perseverance and skill, combined with the tools available to contemporary quilters, allow perfect piecing with any type of fabric. Machine-quilting has been executed by only a few skilled sewers since the turn of the century. However, during the 1980s sewing machines became more sophisticated. Many adjustments in tensions and pressure were now possible and an abundant variety of attachments became available for the serious sewer. Machine-quilting has gradually become popular and can be well executed by a skilled sewer. This quilt attests to the fact that simple machine-quilting can be done with any fabric.

Galactic Gears 1990
Thunder Bay, Ontario
Jackie Black

Detail of **V-Pattern** *block*

New fabric was seldom purchased for a quilt being made for home use. However, the maker of this vibrant Scrap quilt had to augment her supplies with packs of cuttings from a nearby shirt factory. This distinctive quilt is a wonderful example of how ingenious quilters were when it came to creating an effect with the resources at hand. Study this design and you will see that the background units have been carefully matched so that they appear to be a uniform colour.

The design is created by assembling four blocks; these blocks become the design block. Considerable care had to be taken when cutting the template pieces, as all the units are tapered. If the cutting and piecing were not reasonably accurate, the design units would not match when the blocks were being assembled. This is a wonderful example of almost perfect piecing—with 12 seams intersecting at

the centres, it is almost impossible to have a perfect match and also keep the block square.

The design has been double bordered and even the inner border has been pieced from assorted scraps. The binding is the backing turned to the front.

This quilter obviously took great pride in her finished work, as she marked a feathered quilting design throughout the central area and quilted a vertical grid in the border. Unfortunately, the quilting does not show on the pattern side, but undoubtedly this quilt would be turned and the reverse side enjoyed even though many of the pencil lines are still visible today.

Heaters were not an option in early cars, so it was not uncommon for the family matriarch to cover her lower extremities with a favourite family quilt while out touring on a Sunday afternoon.

V-Pattern *c. 1930, East Zorra Township, Ontario, Katharine Weicker*

MEET THE McQUADE SISTERS

Quilting is very much entrenched in the culture of Ontario. While quilting was an absolute necessity in order to provide bedcovering in the home, it was not all drudgery. Quilting bees afforded busy women an opportunity to socialize and exchange gossip while working on a recently completed top.

The McQuades follow a family tradition. These sisters—Florence, Eunice and Ella—were schooled in the art of quilting by their mother, Phyllis McQuade, and grandmother Virginia Dashineau. They had a happy home life, busy as it was with seven girls and two boys needing to be fed and clothed. Not only did their mother make quilts, she also made all the clothes for her girls! Since commercial clothing patterns were not readily available, she would study the styles in the Eaton's and Simpsons catalogues. After the girls chose their favourites, their mother would proceed to create their clothes while simultaneously creating a pattern. Their father was a carpenter, and the girls can remember him assisting his wife with her quilting patterns. He would draw out the patterns and make any templates that were required for the current project. While it has generally been thought that quilting was a woman's occupation, many husbands were very proud and supportive of their wives' talents. They would use their skills to create quilting frames, ornate C-clamps and other paraphernalia which could be enjoyed by the women in their households.

Crazy *c. 1890*
Barrie, Ontario
Ella Ruth

As a child, Florence enjoyed quilting with her mother. Her mother owned a sewing machine, so most of the piecing was done by machine, but she still had no time for quilting bees. When their mother was quilting, the girls had an opportunity to visit with her. Florence has many fond memories of happy hours of fellowship with her mother at the quilting frame. Quilting for many women was a time of relaxation and therapy after long hours of running busy, active households with numerous children.

Unlike Florence, Eunice did not have a great interest in quilting as a child. Rather, she enjoyed sewing clothes or socializing with her friends. However, she also enjoyed many quiet hours with her mother after an evening out with friends. Her mother quietly sewed or quilted while waiting for the children to come home.

Ella was a busy child and really had no interest in needle skills until after she was married, at which time she began sewing for her family. However, she did acquire basic skills in her mother's home. After Ella's own family was grown, and the sisters gradually migrated back to their birthplace, she became interested in quilting with her sisters.

These sisters come from a long line of quilters, including their mother and grandmother as well as a very special aunt, Ella, who also came from a prolific family of sewers and quilters. While all the family quilts were made to be used, it is interesting to see that they have been carefully cared for and treasured by the family members. These tactile objects conjure up many emotions and stories of bygone events.

Crazy quilts were made to be viewed and treasured. They were seldom slept under, rather they were more often displayed on a sofa for all to enjoy while

*Detail of **Crazy** quilt on page 44 showing embroidery and feather-stitching*

participating in a singalong. Family times were special times in the McQuade household. They enjoyed many happy hours gathered around the piano singing while their older brother played. Crazy quilts are a medley of carefully assembled scraps, and here the sisters can be seen reminiscing over some favourite medleys. Gracing the piano are pictures of their now deceased great-grandmother, Susannah Trotter McQuade; their maternal grandmother, Virginia Dashineau; and their parents, Phyllis and Charles McQuade, with four of their children.

Quilts and music were always important elements in the lives of the McQuade women, and here we see Aunt Ella's quilt displayed on the piano. Like all quilts created by the McQuades, it was

made from scraps acquired from Aunt Gertie, who was a renowned dressmaker in the area. Some of the units are beautifully embellished with intricate embroidery. True to tradition, a skilled needle-woman would embroider the scraps together using as many embroidery stitches as she knew. The more stitches and threads, the more admired the needlewoman, and the more cherished the quilt. The quilt is now owned by Ella, who is very proud of her aunt's talents.

Here we see a mother-and-daughter pair of quilts. Phyllis McQuade instilled in her girls a great love for traditional designs, and on the bed there is a red-and-white Double Irish Chain made recently by Ella. Ella chose to use a bright red-and-white print for her design, which gives the quilt a soft viewing line. She used a 1-inch grid for the quilting. When combined with the polycotton batting, which became available in the 1980s, we see considerable loft to the surface of a favoured quilt.

At the foot of the bed is one of Phyllis's last quilts, Love Ring, which is a variation of the Drunkard's Path. Phyllis set her blocks together to create a quilt with four Love Ring blocks. The design is easy to arrange once a central circle has been started. The quilter can add as many rings as she chooses. Upon careful inspection, you will observe that Phyllis turned one of her squares the wrong way. Sometimes this was done deliberately; sometimes it was an error. She also liked to contain her design within a border, and here she has used a simple half-square border motif. Phyllis used cotton batting in her quilt and quilted it with a 2-inch grid. It is easy to see that the larger the quilting grid, the less loft to the surface of the quilt. Also, with cotton batting, which has a tendency to mat when washed and dried unless closely quilted, a quilt will become very flat and uneven after even a few washings. If you look carefully here you will notice that this has already happened.

Double Irish Chain 1987
Barrie, Ontario
Phyllis McQuade
Drunkard's Path c. 1942
Barrie, Ontario
Phyllis McQuade

Susannah McQuade enjoyed piecing; the numerous squares and triangles have been perfectly handpieced. Considering that much of the work would have been completed by lamplight, she must have had excellent eyesight. Two-colour quilts were very popular. Red and white was a particular favourite because it kept its colour through repeated washings and years of use.

The blocks have been sashed with a design known as Garden Maze, which not only outlines each block but also gives considerable movement to the design. The batting used in this quilt was thin cotton which has mostly disintegrated with wear. It is quite likely that this was a spring-summer quilt used by the parents and/or guests, since it has been created from small blocks and would have been very time-consuming to

Double-X c. 1895
Barrie, Ontario
Susannah McQuade

create. Like many quilts of the era, it has been quilted using a clamshell design, a popular quilting pattern.

Hole-in-the-Barn-Door 1958
Barrie, Ontario
Ella Gauthier

What a wonderful and productive place to visit—around the quilting frame which has been located near a well-lit window. Here the sisters are quilting on Florence's appliqué quilt, which has been created from old bleached flour sacks. It is always a task of the hostess to have a supply of threaded needles ready in the pincushion clamp which is affixed to the frame. This allows the quilters to keep quilting and not lose their rhythm by having to stop to thread needles. However, there is always a spool of thread on the quilt should the sisters need to replenish their needles during the afternoon.

An afternoon spent around the quilting frame provides the sisters with an opportunity to catch up on family happenings and any other snippets of news. These sisters, who were taught by their mother, grandmother and aunts, started sewing and quilting at a very early age, and now that they are all back living in the same area, they are able to get together and quilt whenever an opportunity presents itself.

In the background on the quilt rack we see a Hole-in-the-Barn-Door quilt created by Ella. It is being displayed for guests to admire.

On this rope bed we see two of Phyllis McQuade's quilts. With such a large family to care for, Phyllis never threw out any fabric. The white circles on the bed quilt were cut from the back of a Dresden Plate quilt and saved for future use. They have been appliquéd onto the blue foundation. Once again, the blue underneath the circles was cut away and used in another project. The red centres add a sense of whimsy to the quilt on the child's bed. The companion Snowball quilt rests across the pillows, just as you might have seen it had you visited the McQuade family home. It is a variation of Drunkard's Path.

Folded over the chair is a colourful Nine-patch variation that was purchased by the owner of the Bittersweet Bed and Breakfast, where it is displayed and welcomes all visitors. It has a Windmill centre accented with red woollen yarn used to tie the quilt. The top has been handpieced with clothing scraps, and a lightweight woollen blanket has been used as batting. This quilt was meant for decoration and the mellow colours complement the two McQuade quilts featured on the bed. Since farm homes in the early nineteenth century had little storage space, it was not uncommon to see quilts draped over a chair such as this one, so that they could be used as needed.

The child's quilt hanging from the antique sled was purchased by the owners of this restored 1830s heritage home. Like many antiques, it is well worn, but now has a place of honour at the top of a child's bed.

Windmill Nine-patch Medallion
Alma, Michigan;
Snowball c. 1942
Barrie, Ontario, Phyllis McQuade
Dresden Plate Backs c. 1949
Barrie, Ontario, Phyllis McQuade

Pennsylvania Dutch Sampler *1987*
Stroud, Ontario
Eunice McLeod

Eunice enjoys appliqué, as it is something she can work on during the summer months while sitting and visiting with family and friends who visit at her lakeside home. Many of the design elements for this quilt came from a purchased Sandy Small pattern. Eunice made alterations to the pattern's layout and colour scheme. Since Eunice is a perfectionist, she took the time to cut out all the background layers of fabric in the appliqué so that there would be no shading through of colours. In order to enhance the design, she also did embroidery work on the peacocks and on some of the finer stems.

Eunice wanted to make a traditional Pennsylvania Dutch Sampler, so the quilting is also simple crosshatching with outline quilting around the design units and minimal stitching within some of the elements for texture and colour. The prints and colours chosen for the design are all typical of such a Sampler. Eunice has successfully captured the feel of Pennsylvania Dutch folklore with her piecing and quilting motifs.

In this beautifully restored 1850s sitting room, complete with authentic stencil designs on the wall, we see a collection of red-and-green quilts displayed for Christmas. Red is a colour used in many heritage quilts, as it was one of the first stable colours.

Turkey red, known as "madder" dyeing, originated in India. From there it was passed along to other parts of the East, including Turkey, where it derived its name and was carried to Europe by the French. Turkey red became the most sought-after colour of the nineteenth century. The process of dyeing was very complicated and required a total of 40 to 50 days to complete. In 1840 the Merrimack and Hamilton Mills in Lowell, Massachusetts, produced more than 250,000 yards of cotton fabrics dyed or printed in madder colours. Many of the fabrics sold in Canada during the nineteenth and twentieth centuries were imported from the United States. These fabrics became relatively easy to acquire in areas where high-quality fabrics were sold.

The Paper Cut quilt in the foreground was made by Sarah E. McNairn at age 12. The appliqué work was done with an almost invisible stitch, and the quilting utilizes a half-inch grid which incorporates feather sprays in the open areas. Here we see that needle skills were very important and learned at an early age by many young girls during the nineteenth century. Sarah was born in 1848 and lived a long life. This quilt would undoubtedly have been part of her trousseau.

The Carolina Lily quilt immediately behind also makes use of turkey red fabric. The appliqué is much finer and exemplifies work done by an accomplished needle-woman. Margaret Laura Quantz had considerable spare time, as her husband was involved in community affairs, so she actively

Christmas Sampler 1987, Stroud, Ontario, Eunice McLeod; *Christmas Sampler* 1987, Barrie, Ontario, Florence Wright; *Carolina Lily* c. 1890, Markham Township, Ontario, Margaret Laura Quantz; *Paper Cut Appliqué* c. 1870, eastern Ontario, Sarah E. McNairn

pursued her needle and quilting endeavours. It is not known exactly how many quilts Margaret made during her busy life (1852-1922), but it is assumed that this one was made in the late 1890s. The Carolina Lily must have been a favourite design for Margaret, since she constructed 20 blocks which were then sashed with the same turkey red. Four small leaves were appliquéd in every intersection and it was then intricately quilted, echoing the floral motif. It is quite possible that this quilt was constructed from new material, since it was probably created for a very special occasion with the design in mind.

The McQuade sisters have both

made Christmas quilts. Eunice's, in the left foreground, is a bold and graphic Sampler wrapped with a large red bow in each corner. Florence, on the other hand, collected some Christmas scenes from a pattern kit. She then used her imagination and scraps to create a Christmas quilt, employing the pattern kit as the inspiration for her blocks. The blocks are bordered with holly leaves, which further enhance the Christmas motif. Upon its completion, Florence gave this quilt to her daughter for enjoyment during the festive season.

Christmas brings families and friends together in warm, cheery settings, and here visitors are

welcomed by a glowing fire and numerous antique Christmas decorations. What a wonderful environment in which to celebrate the spirit of Christmas!

The quilts in this room are part of the McQuade collection. On the bed we see a Dresden Fan quilt with the blocks assembled in opposing directions. The quilt was made from dress and apron scraps, as were many of the McQuade quilts. Aunt Ella had acquired an indelible pen and dated this quilt before she quilted it. Dating was not commonly done and was certainly not done with pen. It is not known why Ella chose to date this particular quilt.

The quilt was made during the Depression, when fabric was scarce and of poor quality. However, it has many bright and attractive prints which probably predate the Depression. Some of the plain fabrics were of poorer quality and have faded. Observe the quilting: all McQuade quilts were made to be used, but Auntie wanted to make this one a little different. She did the quilting in straight lines, in opposite directions which do not intersect. By using simple quilting lines, she has given this quilt a very simplistic welcoming charm.

A Honeycomb quilt rests over the foot of the bed, just waiting to be used. The "honeycomb" set was very popular and was given different names in different areas. This configuration was often known as Canadian Conventional Star or Colonial Flower Garden.

Dresden Fan 1934
Barrie, Ontario, Ella Ruth
Honeycombe c. 1935
Barrie, Ontario, Phyllis McQuade

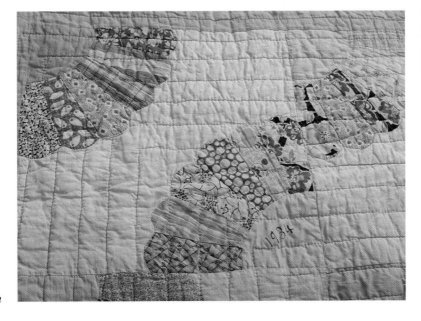

Detail of **Dresden Fan**

Kaleidoscope *1987*
Barrie, Ontario
Florence Wright

Chimney Sweep c. 1900
Barrie, Ontario
Ella Ruth

In 1982 the newly formed Canadian Quilters' Association held its first national conference and the McQuade sisters were in attendance. Florence took a Kaleidoscope workshop taught by Polly Greene of Nova Scotia. The participants were instructed to bring an assortment of scraps and were then encouraged to trade scraps to increase the number of fabrics available. Florence traded around and here we see her completed quilt.

Kaleidoscope is a design which appears to be circular, but the whole top is created using two different sizes of triangles. The careful placement of fabric colours and quilting creates a circular illusion.

The Chimney Sweep Scrap quilt was made by Aunt Ella, who certainly enjoyed handstitching. It is completely handpieced and handquilted with a clamshell design, a favourite of quilters because it softens the linear effect of the piecing. Aunt Ella enjoyed spending many relaxing hours piecing and quilting near a sunny window, where she could admire the scenery. This quilt was photographed in the yard among the early blooms of spring, which she always loved.

As mentioned, all McQuade quilts were made to be used. This regular use necessitated laundering of the quilts. The solid green and green-print fabrics were not made from stable dyes and have lightened significantly with repeated laundering and exposure to light.

STAR QUILTS

Lone Star, pieced on two sides, origin unknown

Church at Ball's Falls

Back of Lone Star

Shapes used in quilts were often similar to those found in architecture and in nature. Graphics were kept simple, as tools for craftspeople and artisans were themselves simple and easy to use. A quilter's tools consisted of a sewing machine (which would only sew straight lines), needles and thread. Patterns were also available. The quilter would carefully trace them onto template material, either cardboard or tin,

and would probably make more than one quilt from any given pattern.

Lone Star was a favoured design among more experienced quilters. It requires careful cutting and piecing, otherwise the quilt will not lie flat. Nothing is known about the quilter of this two-sided quilt which was purchased at an auction in 1985. However, it is interesting to observe how skilled she was with her fabrics. The points do *not* all have the same

fabrics in them. Through careful use of colour, the quilter was able to create a very pleasing design which has been quilted with a diagonal grid.

Perhaps this quilter liked variety. She echoed the piecing design on the back. Undoubtedly, this quilt was also used with the back side up, probably during the bright sunny months, since the fabrics used in the Lone Star are still vibrant.

The lively Prairie Star quilt was pieced and quilted in the Maritimes. Many of the settlers in Nova Scotia emigrated from Great Britain, where needling was very much a part of their lifestyle.

Stars are difficult to cut and piece so that the finished quilt will lie flat and be square. While design and colour were important, the early quilters often had to compromise slightly on straight sides. However, these quilts were always used on beds and a little distortion went unnoticed. This quilt has been carefully hand-pieced and has withstood many years of constant use.

Prairie Star *c. 1880, The Maritimes*

Stars were favoured by the quilter who handpieced this exquisite quilt. Each star is less than 3 inches from point to point, and so required careful cutting and piecing of the star sections. Like many quilts, this is a Scrap quilt which was carefully planned and pieced. Each unit of seven stars was pieced and fitted into the overall design. The quilter lived in Indiana at the time she made this complex quilt. Fabric must have been scarce, as the muslin used is not all from the same dye lot and the back is also seamed.

This quilt has been much used and enjoyed by its owners and is now showing some signs of light damage. One area of yellow-and-brown-striped stars has faded to a uniform beige-and-brown strip. The quilt was intended for warmth, as it has a woollen batting which can be seen at the edges where some of the fabric has worn through, probably from being tucked repeatedly under the mattress.

The clamshell quilting has been carefully executed with small uniform stitches which with years of laundering give the surface a textured appearance.

Red-sprigged muslin was a favourite of quilters and was used by this quilter for her binding. It also serves to frame the central design, as there are no borders.

Seven Stars for Seven Sisters
Paola, Indiana
Mrs. Dibble

Feathered Stars c. 1900
Mount Forest, Ontario
Ann Morton and Eliza Smith Evans

Ann and Eliza were sisters-in-law and both were accomplished needlewomen. This Feathered Star quilt has been totally handpieced. To further accentuate each star, each ray of the central white star has been embroidered with red thread, while each block has been sashed with numerous small diamonds. The little diamonds enhance the star contained therein while adding to the jaggedness of the star's rays.

This quilt has been quilted very closely with exceedingly small stitches on a diagonal grid. While it is now owned by a fourth-generation Smith, it is still in excellent condition. It was probably made as a special quilt and has been cared for accordingly. The sisters did have some trouble with their piecing, setting some of the feathered units into the star backwards. However, this quilt was made before electricity was in-vented and homes were consider-ably darker inside. Errors such as this often were not noticed until after a block was pieced, and they were usually not corrected. For-tunately, when a quilt is lying on a bed, you do not see all the stars at once, so mistakes often remain unnoticed.

Lone Star *c. 1910*
origin unknown

Lone Star quilts were only attempted by experienced quilters. They require careful cutting and piecing, otherwise the star will be misshapen and the quilt will not lie flat. This quilter chose to use a fairly large diamond, 3 inches per side, and to carefully seam the quilt by hand. While little is known about the quilter, this was probably one of her early attempts with this pattern. It has been quilted with a simple block grid in the open areas and outline quilting for the star.

The choice of colours is par- ticularly pleasing. This was probably a special quilt in a western Ontario home. Certainly it is treasured by its current owner, who undoubtedly has a large bed on which to display it.

Star quilts have long been a favourite for piecers. On the bed is a perfectly pieced Scrap Star of Bethlehem quilt. The satellite stars have been pieced from the same scrap fabrics as the central star.

Hazel Graham pieced her quilt during the 1930s, when fabrics were scarce and quilters were challenged to be creative with their scraps. The colours in this quilt give it a spring-like flair. Pictured here in a restored 1830s master bedroom, the quilt has been displayed with folk-art Easter decorations and a 1903 Harvest Sun quilt made in Jensig, New Brunswick, but never used.

Rachel Carmichael of New Brunswick dyed the gold fabric for her Harvest Sun quilt using the blossoms of the marsh marigolds which were common in her area. Rachel was especially creative when it came to quilting; she chose to use concentric circles rather than the usual linear design. She then bordered her finished quilt with the same gold fabric which she used for her design. While the quilt was made in 1903, the dye used is remarkably stable and remains a vibrant shade of yellow.

Star of Bethlehem c. 1930 (on bed), Lindsey, Ontario, Hazel Graham
Harvest Sun c. 1903, Jensig, New Brunswick, Rachel Carmichael

years, it will have to be treated with special care.

The quilter's name has been lost to history, but she took great pride in her work, as illustrated by her pieced satellite stars. Between all the star points she used only green print fabric. This quilt is a good example of how well the colour "turkey red" will retain its intensity through repeated washings and usage. The quilter did some elaborate quilting within the inner border, and the remainder of the top has just been gridded. To preserve the edges of this heirloom, about 20 years ago the owner added a border of blending fabric and quilted it.

Lone Star c. 1889, Groveton, Ontario, Emily Tanney and Mary Jane Coville

Quilts were frequently given as wedding presents, which made them cherished items. Emily Tanney and Mary Jane Coville made this one as their gift for their sister, Sarah Jane Phelps, at the time of her marriage in 1889. The star has been all handpieced. It would be interesting to know whether the sisters became accomplished machine-piecers after Sarah's marriage, as her husband, Mr. Phelps, travelled the country selling sewing machines!

This quilt has been enjoyed by several generations and laundered so often that the cotton batting has almost totally disintegrated. However, the fabrics are still vibrant in colour. The mustard yellow which was so popular as a quilting fabric colour was also a popular colour for paint pigments. A housewife would use every opportunity to add a little colour to an otherwise drab room.

A common sight in the country was the rain barrel. Water was collected from the roof and used for laundry and bathing. It was a precious commodity in most rural communities, as wells frequently dried up in the summer. Laundry was then kept to a minimum and the rain water was saved and used for cooking.

The Star of Bethlehem quilt has a wonderful assortment of eighteenth-century block prints, many of which are still vivid. Two of the prints had dyes that were not very stable and are badly faded. Rot has also set into some of the patches. Although this wonderful early example of Canadiana has been enjoyed by family members for almost 200

Star of Bethlehem c. 1800
Pennsylvania

59

The Fee family moved to the St. Catharines area from Tiverton, Bruce County, around 1890 to engage in fruit farming. The three Fee girls never married and would rendezvous at the family farm, where Ann lived and kept house for her brother. There they would visit and quilt. After Henrietta and Jen retired from the work force, all four Fees would winter in Texas and Mexico. It is quite possible that they saw the pattern for this particular Star variation while on holiday.

Shirting fabric was used for the piecing of the stars, while red-sprigged muslin was used for the squares. It is likely that one sister did all of the piecing and then the three sisters quilted together during the winter months. A quilting frame was always set up in the parlour in the St. Catharines farmhouse. It is interesting to note that the stars recede into the background, and the secondary design of whirling squares comes forward since the red used is such a dominant colour. A different selection of fabrics would have made another very interesting Star quilt.

Detail of **LeMoyne Star** *blocks*

LeMoyne Star *c. 1920*
St. Catharines, Ontario
The Fee Sisters

Ohio Star c. 1882
Vineland, Ontario

Stars, sky and ground were common elements to quilters. The fabrics for this quilt, dated 1882, were probably purchased at the general store in Jordan and are similar to those used in the pieced quilts on page 38. Browns and blues must have been popular colours in this farming community at the time, as all of these quilts and their backs have solids and prints in similar shades.

On a breezy, overcast day, it was not unusual to see quilts that were too large to hang on a clothesline lying on the ground airing. Airing was important because farmhouses were heated with wood stoves which created considerable dust and soot. During spring housecleaning, quilts would be shaken, beaten, laundered or aired, depending on the fabrics.

This Ohio Star quilt has been perfectly pieced and a simple horizontal grid was used as a quilting motif. Each block was quilted "in the ditch" (in the seam line), accentuating the fact that the squares were placed on the point when the quilt was being assembled.

Looking at this quilt resting on the grass, it is easy to understand why some shades of blue are referred to as "sky blue."

CRAZY QUILTS

Crazy 1885, Mersea Township, Ontario, Nettie Windsor

This unique form of patchwork became popular during the Victorian era and lasted until World War I. Crazy quilting is really a form of fabric collage that served as a showcase for the creator's skill with fancy needlework. The irregularly shaped scraps were pieced together on a foundation fabric using a variety of embroidery stitches. Additional embroidery embellishments, which were frequently spectacular, were often worked on some of the patches. Sometimes the assorted scraps were assembled into blocks which were also joined using embroidery stitches. Periodically, blocks would be sashed, forming a grid to contain their kinetic activity.

Many Crazy quilts were constructed as tops and, in this case, the foundation fabric, probably muslin or unbleached cotton, was one piece. While these tops are always referred to as Crazy quilts, this is really a misnomer, as they have no stitching to hold the layers together. Technically, they are coverlets. It is also interesting to observe that many quilters chose to tie these quilts carefully with knots to the back, so as not to detract from the embroidery.

The favourite materials for Crazy quilts were silks, velvets, jacquards, brocades, satins and taffetas, either new or salvaged from worn-out garments or home furnishings. The quilts were not meant to be used on an everyday basis and were generally found adorning a sofa in the parlour, on the top of the grand piano, or as a throw on a guest bed, to be removed before retiring.

In rural areas, well into the early 1900s, plain Crazy quilts were being made with lightweight wools and homespuns. The woollen scraps were carefully embroidered together, and most Crazy quilts were used infrequently by special guests during the cold winters. Like their more elaborate counterparts, they were also used as throws to satisfy the desire for something colourful.

Crazy quilts also became "memory" quilts. The dates of important family events and other momentous occasions were often embroidered on different patches. The Crazy quilts that survive remain as a testament to the creativity and needle skills of many of Ontario's pioneer women.

Embroidery was a skill taught to most young girls in England. It was expected that all "refined" English ladies be accomplished needlewomen. The Crazy quilt afforded the proud bourgeois lady an opportunity to display her talents for all to admire. It is interesting to note that many of these artifacts have dates and signatures worked into them. They were really meant to be enjoyed and passed on to succeeding generations. Indeed, this book is a testament to the fact that many quilts have been treated as special family heirlooms and given utmost care by several generations of a family.

Crazy quilts were much loved and appreciated by those who had the ability to make them, as well as by their admirers, who would give these needlers pieces of cherished or expensive fabrics left over from their sewing projects.

Nettie Windsor was born in Mersea Township, Ontario, and was related to the Fosters who emigrated from England and settled in the Leamington area. Ralph Foster was one of the founders of the town of Leamington, and his progeny remained in the area. Nettie was also related to the Jacksons who founded a furniture and china store in Leamington in 1887. The quilt seen on page 62 is adorned with family mementos and other Victorian pictures. It has been used periodically in displays in the family store and

Crazy, Creemore, Ontario

was featured during their centennial celebrations.

Nettie never married. She lived with her sister during her later years, so she had considerable time to devote to her sewing and embroidery endeavours. Like many creators of Crazy quilts, she was sufficiently proud of her work to date this piece.

By the late nineteenth century, life was becoming easier for some women. They were now established in comfortable homes and communities, and they could enjoy some of the amenities of the times. Many owned sewing machines. General stores carried sewing supplies, and quilting bees were common.

Nothing is known about the quilt shown on this page, except that it was bought at an auction in Creemore in 1985. However, the quilter had a sense of humour. You can read captions such as "stick me," "hide that blot," "wet laundry," "baby's album," "duster bag" and many others. Her embroidery skills were impeccable. The quilt was made entirely from sturdy colour co-ordinated upholstery velvets and velours. It was then quilted to a cotton chintz backing. Since the quilt is still in mint condition, it was probably never used by the maker.

Detail showing embroidery motifs used on ***Crazy***

Crazy quilts are a medley of fabric scraps, textures, embroidery and designs. Unfortunately, nothing is known about the history of this quilt, which is dated 1891. We see that the quilter liked the Baby's Block pattern, as she appliquéd a Pandora's Box block unit onto one of the elements. There is also a block with a crown and British flag, which reveals a British affiliation. Examples of exquisite embroidery on many units show the skills of a master needle-woman. The pieces have been embroidered together using many types of embroidery stitches, and the unique prairie-point border of velvet has been feather-stitched on all sides.

The back of this quilt has been quilted to batting and then sewn to the top. Generally, Crazy quilts were tied to the batting and back-ing. However, a top worked as ex-tensively as this one was meant to be seen by all. The quilter took great pride in her work, thus the back had to be as carefully finished as the front.

The quilt is seen resting over the back of an Empire sofa, as you would see it in a well-appointed home.

While Crazy quilts have been a way of displaying one's creative skills since the late 1800s, it is quite likely that this quilt was a learning experience for a child. The embroidery has a juvenile theme and, while it has been well executed, the stitches are basic ones. Since the embroidery is very sparse, it is possible that the child tired of the project and some adult bound it with black velvet, tied it to the back with burgundy wool-len yarn, and kept it as a keepsake.

Crazy 1891, origin unknown

Crazy
Chicago, Illinois
Mrs. A. Hammer

Crazy 1883
Amherstburg, Ontario
Annie Foster Hyatt

Details above and below showing date and embroidery designs

In 1812 Canada declared its Black residents to be "free." As word of this travelled south through the United States, Black slaves fled north via the "Underground Railroad." Prior to the American Civil War, this "railroad" was a system by which slaves were secretly assisted in their escape to the free states or to Canada. During the 1830s and 1840s many "terminals" were set up along the shores of Lake Erie and the Niagara River, and the fleeing slaves were ferried into Canada by the side-wheel paddle steamers travelling between the United States and Canada.

Here we have a dated 1883 Crazy quilt made by Annie Foster Hyatt and her grandmothers. Levi Foster, Annie's father, was a tavern owner in Amherstburg and undoubtedly his tavern would have been a meeting place for many of the area's Black people. Many former slave women would have acquired some of their embroidery skills by observing their White owners or by looking at pictures from current embroidery publications that were available to them.

As you study the collection of quilts in this section, it is interesting to note the similarity of many of the designs. Most are embellished with a variety of embroidery motifs. All the embellishments in this quilt are objects seen in everyday life. They are worked and enhanced by a skilful use of embroidery threads and stitches.

The styles of the Victorian era afforded skilled needlewomen an outlet for their design and embroidery talents. Margaret Hume was born in Scotland and practised tailoring and dressmaking after she immigrated to Ingersoll. The family must have had a special interest in canoeing because sewn into this quilt are two ribbons from the Brantford Canoe Club, dated 1892 and 1893, and a ribbon dated 1885 from the Canadian Wheelsmen Association. It is quite likely that the fabric scraps used were scraps from Margaret's clients. Many of the units have been further embellished with embroidery motifs, probably copied from an embroidery booklet that she purchased, or perhaps from one sent to her from Scotland as a gift.

Canoeing has long been a popular recreational activity in Ontario. Here we see an early crude dugout canoe carved from a large old tree.

Crazy c. 1885
Ingersoll, Ontario
Margaret Hume

Women enjoyed having an opportunity to display their needle skills. The origin of this cloth is unknown, but the needle-woman used her sewing and embroidery skills with finesse when she chose to make a tea cloth utilizing some of her more precious scraps.

Tea was a daily afternoon ritual during the late nineteenth and early twentieth century. Here the cloth graces a typical English tea table that is set and awaiting the arrival of guests.

Like many Crazy quilts, these are actually coverlets, as there is no batting or quilting. It is interesting to observe that both women chose to make useful table-coverings rather than throws from their scraps.

Crazy Edged Table Cover c. 1880
Stanstead, Québec, Caroline Dickerson

Afternoon tea was a time for socializing, when time permitted. Caroline Dickerson was one of eight children born to Silas and Mary Dickerson of Stanstead, Québec. She was born in 1830 and lived to age 66. During her busy lifetime she was able to create a number of interesting pieces of needlework. In order to preserve her embroidery, this crazy work was done as a border which was then applied to a central square of felt. The corners have received special treatment; Caroline took strips from her assortment of silks, taffetas and velvets and worked them in a fan shape around each of the four corners.

Crazy Edged Table Cover
origin unknown

Crazy quilts *reading left to right:*
Top only c. 1908, Forest, Ontario;
c. 1880, Lynden, Ontario;
c. 1900, Port Hope, Ontario

Crazy quilts were popular for about 30 years. The designers of the quilts pictured here did not have a large inventory of exotic fabrics. The upper and lower quilts have some velvet, but most of the fabrics used were suitings. The embroidery is uniform in all the quilts, but the quilters either did not have the skill or the expertise to do the surface embroidery on the patches that was so typical of Crazy quilts of the late nineteenth century.

The quilter of the centre quilt was of English extraction. She chose to make her quilt of knit fabric, probably brought with her from England. The embroidery is well executed and this quilt is an interesting study of fabrics. However, it is unfortunate that the fabric was not durable and has not withstood wear and tear over the years.

Most farm homes had a day bed such as this one found in the sitting room of the Ball home in Jordan. A Crazy quilt would probably have been displayed and used by guests.

Memory Quilt *c. 1891*
origin unknown

The owners of this quilt consider it a Memory quilt since it contains many personal family mementos. Little is known about the quilter, but the owners purchased this treasure in 1960. However, in the embroidery you can read phrases such as "Stockport, London"; "to our brave volunteers 1885"; "Windermere Aug. 1881"; "T.C.C."; "H.R. Tilley, Toronto 1889"; "R.S.W."; "finished 1891." One can only speculate as to whether this quilt was made in England and subsequently brought to Canada, or whether the ribbons were collected in England, brought to this country, and the quilt made here.

The quilter chose to work her mementos on eight large blocks which, when completed, she masterfully sewed together. The back was quilted with burgundy thread in a clamshell design. It was then tied to the top with yellow ribbon, which blends in with the embroidery while simultaneously giving additional interest to the back.

As was typical of the Victorian era, the more embroidery stitches used on the quilt, the more accomplished the needlewoman. Upon examining this quilt, you will see that many of the pieces have been embroidered with fanciful designs, attesting to the fact that most bourgeois English-women were very skilled embroiderers.

LOG CABIN QUILTS

Pineapple Variation c. 1880, probably made in central Ontario

og Cabin quilts are one of the most meaningful styles because of the central importance of the home to life on the frontier. They portray a visual abstraction of pioneer homes. The light side faces the sun and the dark side evokes night. This design transcends time and lifestyles. To this day, it is still a very popular pattern, as it allows flexibility with colour and set. During the opulence of the Victorian era, Log Cabin quilts were made using many silks and velvets, creating a richness in texture and design which could not have been achieved with cottons.

The basic block is very simple, starting with a small central square. Generally, this square was red to portray the warmth of the hearth. If it was yellow, it portrayed the light in a window, a welcome to a weary traveller. A narrow strip, equal in length to the side of the square, is joined to one edge of the centre square to form a rectangle. The next strip, equal in width to the preceeding one but longer, is joined to the long edge of the rectangle. Succeeding strips, always the same width but progressively longer, are attached around the rectangles until the block is the desired size.

Variations in patterns are created through the positioning of colour as the block is being built up. The completed blocks are then assembled in a predetermined order to create the chosen design.

Log Cabin quilts were a favourite of the travelling seamstresses who moved from home to home, sewing the year's clothing for other families. On occasion, such a woman was fortunate enough to be allowed to keep the scraps which were new, unwashed, of good quality and assorted variety. She would be able to use the tiniest of pieces in the logs of her quilt. Hence these quilts have an extremely interesting variety of fabrics.

Log Cabin quilts have many sets and are generally very graphic. This 1880 much-worn Pineapple Variation quilt was found nailed to a barn wall, where it was used as a television backdrop.

The logs are constructed from an assortment of cotton and woollen fabrics, with the central squares in the traditional red. However, we see a secondary striped square appear when the blocks are pieced, which gives this design an added dimension.

On cloudy days, quilts which were too heavy to be hung on a clothesline would be aired over mature bushes. This quilt has not had the best of care and is seen here as it is just starting to slip off the bushes during an early spring airing.

Here, in the living room of this restored farm manor, is a collection of Log Cabin quilts which symbolizes the lifestyle of the residents in a late nineteenth-century manor home.

Log Cabin quilts were made with any type of scrap from the scrap bag. The scraps were sorted into lights and darks. A block size and possibly a set were decided upon. These four quilts exemplify the masterful use of colour and scraps. It has been said that "necessity is the mother of invention" and the pioneer women certainly found numerous arrangements for their Log Cabin blocks.

The Sunshine and Shadow quilt over the fireplace was purchased by the Edwards. It gives a feeling of warmth and coziness to this drawing room. It has been constructed using a symmetrical block with red at its centre. These centres look like jewels scattered throughout the design.

In the background is a colourful quilt whose set is Barn Raising (c. 1910). Its light logs have been created from a great variety of scraps. Since the centre squares are not the usual red, the dark lines of the dark side of the block become the focus for the set. This quilt was created by a mother-and-daughter team, Maude and Margaret Swazye of the Niagara Peninsula, using suitings and the odd piece of cotton. Some of the light logs were cut from a white-and-brown leaf print which was sewn over a burgundy-and-white print that peeks out in a few spots. When Maude and Margaret were setting the blocks together, they decided that the brown-and-white print provided a better visual effect. This quilt has been hand-pieced over a heavy foundation and has a gathered binding. This heirloom was probably made for a guest bed and considered a "good" quilt.

In contrast, the quilt in the right foreground (c. 1940) has a similar variety of colours in the light logs, but the centres of each block are the traditional red. This, combined with a fold in each log, provides a highly dimensional graphic quilt. At the time, many suiting fabrics were purchased by the pound from a nearby garment factory. The extra fabric in each log, along with the fold, makes the quilt quite heavy. Consequently, these quilts were primarily used in extremely cold weather and were not subjected to prolonged use.

The quilt in the left foreground (c. 1920) makes random use of scraps. While the logs are generally a dark assortment of suitings, flannel and dark velvets, they are not as uniform in colour density as in the other three quilts. Nor was any effort made to control the use of the colours in the light scraps, some of which are light sateen lining fabrics.

All of these quilts were certainly made to be used. Surprisingly, they are all in reasonably good condition.

Sunshine and Shadow c. 1900 (over the mantle), origin unknown; *Barn Raising* c. 1910 (over chair in background), Niagara Peninsula, Ontario, Maude and Margaret Swazye; *Streak O' Lightning* c. 1920 (over chair in foreground), origin unknown; *Straight Furrows* c. 1940, Niagara Peninsula, Ontario

The McLagan family, with four boys and four girls, immigrated to Canada in June of 1853. They left Scotland on the ship *Cameo* and were six weeks at sea. When the ship landed at Québec, two girls came down with the measles and were quarantined on the ship for another ten days. The family then sailed from Québec to Montréal on the *Lord Elgin*, and from Montréal to Hamilton on the *Lady Elgin*. At Hamilton they hired a team of horses to take them to Stratford, where Helen McLagen had a cousin. The trip from Hamilton to Stratford took only two days, but the total journey took in excess of ten weeks.

It is not known where the McLagans lived before they moved into their first house. They arrived by sleigh late at night on New Year's Day 1854. They inhabited a small but well-constructed log cabin which consisted of a "but and ben" (a one-room cabin with a one-room addition) with a partition, and a loft accessed by ladder. No sooner had the men completed building a shelf to hold what few dishes had been brought from Scotland than the family cat jumped on the shelf and brought down all the dishes. The only items saved were a brown jug and a bottle of castor oil!

William worked at an oatmeal mill the first winter and spring. That spring another daughter was born, and William began renting a mill in Stratford, leaving Helen and the family to run the farm. Misfortune began to plague the McLagens. The family cow was killed by a falling timber while they were hauling logs for the Grand Trunk bridge at Mitchell. The following New Year's Day saw the mill flooded, ruining the oats. Then the family had a bad fright when some Natives broke into the house demanding "fire water." The McLagans were rescued by a neighbour who pacified the intruders with ham and bread. Wildcats and bears were plentiful and prowled outside the house at night. The following year another son was born, the mill burned and the family lost all their grain. At the time they had only 20 pounds of flour, which would not last until harvest time.

There were no roads between Stratford and Mitchell, where the family farm was located—only a trail through the bush—so travel between these destinations was slow and hazardous.

During the next few years life gradually improved for the family. They made sufficient money through the combined labours of all family members to turn their efforts towards the making of potash. Eventually, they were able to build the first frame house in the area, which replaced their cramped log cabin.

When we think of pioneer life, we recognize that hardships were a part of everyday existence. Log cabins were *not* always warm, so the women in the family pieced quilts such as this one, with a fold in each log for additional warmth. Not only has the top been pieced from scrap fabrics, but the back is homespun. It was probably made by the women in the family, who were responsible for preparing and weaving of the yarn. To hold the layers of fabric together, the centre square of each block has been quilted with an X. While these quilts were exceedingly warm, they were also very heavy due to the amount of fabric in them. Thus, it is not surprising that as homes became better heated many of these heirlooms were cast aside and forgotten.

Barn Raising, *Stratford, Ontario, a McLagan descendant*

Barn Raising c. 1930
Peterborough County, Ontario
Sarah Barrie

Detail of **Barn Raising**
showing "set" of the blocks

Log Cabin quilts have long been favoured by quilters as a way of using up scraps while creating a family treasure. Generally, these quilts were made with solid colours, but Sarah Barrie chose to use prints for this Barn Raising set. The fabric in the central square is a rayon blend, which gives a sheen to the block. The other fabrics are prints from the 1920s. Note how the red print was only used to accentuate the centre square and the four corners of the first ring.

Sarah did not finish this quilt. It was put away until 1945, when she found it while doing some housecleaning. She gave it to her daughter, Kay, who completed it in 1987. Kay chose to do her quilting with red thread. This creates an interesting pattern in the border and on the back, while giving a contemporary appearance to a colourful antique top.

Barn Raising *c. 1910*
Tiverton, Ontario
Mrs. McLauren

Log Cabin quilts abound in Ontario. In many rural communities the women of the household used the raw wool from sheep raised on the farm to card, comb and spin into yarn.

The red centres of these blocks are made from red wool and the logs are made from suitings. Mrs. McLauren of Tiverton wove the fabric for the backing; it is a fine example of homespun cloth.

This quilt was photographed on a spinning wheel, which was an important appliance in most well-appointed rural homes.

Log Cabin quilts and rope beds are two of Ontario's important historical artifacts. Rope beds were common in rural Ontario and old quilts were often used next to the ropes to keep the feather or straw mattresses from sagging through the ropes, which stretched with use. Here we see the quilt in a child's typical bedroom, complete with rope bed, stencilled chair and fabric doll, all dimly lit by a candle in a wooden holder.

This Log Cabin quilt has light centre squares instead of the usual red or dark centres. As was customary, it is a Scrap quilt made from suitings and linings. Some of the silk and taffeta fabrics have disintegrated. The blocks were sewn over a foundation fabric, which was likewise scrap fabric. As some of the silks have rotted, it is easy to see the foundation fabric that was used.

Log Cabin quilts have been made since the first settlers arrived on Canadian soil. Fabric was scarce in most areas, yet quilts were absolutely necessary for warmth. Many immigrants were unaware of the harshness of an Ontario winter or the difficult lifestyle to which they had come. Some brought clothes of velvets and silks, which were luxurious but not very practical or durable. As these garments became worn, their undamaged sections were cut and used in quilts such as this Log Cabin. The black fabric is velvet, as are some of the other colours. The remainder of the logs are silks and taffetas, most of which are now starting to disintegrate.

The quilt has been all hand-pieced by a number of Hulhall family members and friends in the village of Proton, a small farming community north of Guelph. They emigrated from County Wicklow, Ireland, during the Great Potato Famine of the 1840s. They were farmers in Ireland, and they remained farmers in the New World. Many of their descendants still live in the Proton area. The women used wool for the batting and tied the top to the back with burgundy wool so as not to detract from the design.

Here we see a quilt resting on a junior officer's bed at Fort George in Niagara-on-the-Lake. All officers were required to provide their own furniture and bedding.

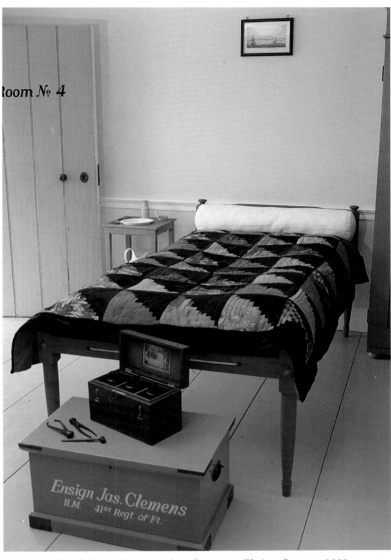

Light and Dark Variation sometimes known as *Flying Geese* c. 1880 Proton, Ontario, a member of the Hulhall family

Barn Raising c. 1903, Stayner, Ontario, Anne Brillinger

A quilt would have been an integral part of an officer's belongings, as it was more than a covering, it was a contact with home and loved ones. We view this quilt on a simple Québec-made rope bed along with the officer's plain trunk, which would have held most of his personal effects. On his trunk we see a travelling gunpowder case complete with tools for pouring the lead and casting the shot.

In a British fort absolutely everything was labelled and inventoried. Hence the trunk and the door of the officer's quarters are clearly labelled.

Open Windows *c. 1900*
possibly central Ontario

A log cabin was home to many early Canadian settlers. These dwellings were usually quite small with few windows, as it was important to keep warm during the winter.

Here we have a variation sometimes known as Open Windows—spring is coming, the snow is almost gone, and a little sunshine presents a welcome opportunity to leave the windows open. Little is known about this quilt, but the quilter apparently wanted high contrast between the light and dark areas to create the illusion of open and closed windows. Like all Log Cabin quilts, it has been made with an assortment of scraps which include some flannelette, some light wools and cottons.

This Log Cabin Sampler, dated 1886, was kept in the Leavens family until 1949, when it was given to its present owner in eastern Ontario as a wedding gift.

This Sampler is made from a collection of silk and taffeta scraps, meticulously embroidered and embellished with maple leaves. It is quite likely that it was originally made as a wedding present. Unfortunately, silks and taffetas rot and many of the logs have begun to disintegrate.

It is interesting to observe that Phoebe Leavens of Hillier chose navy for her sashing, allowing the dark edges of the blocks to be clearly defined while not detracting from the sets. Pheobe had a steady hand and great stamina when it came to using her treadle sewing machine. The embroidery has been done on the sewing machine, and it would have taken considerable practice to move this fabric smoothly through the machine while simultaneously working the treadle. Considering that machine embroidery and quilting was not practised or accepted among quilters until the early 1980s, Phoebe was a century ahead of her time.

Sampler 1886 (*Barn Raising*, centre; *Diamond*, corners; *Court House Steps*, borders)
Prince Edward County, Ontario
Phoebe Leavens

Random Set *c. 1890*
Waterloo County, Ontario

The Log Cabin quilt can be randomly sewn, with little regard as to the placement of colour. Just as the logs in this photograph are randomly piled, so are the blocks of this 1890 quilt, which was probably created in a hurry as winter was approaching and yet another quilt was needed to keep all the family members and guests warm.

This colourful quilt was made in Waterloo County. It is not known whether this is a Mennonite quilt or a winter quilt made from the usual dark fabrics. However, Waterloo County is home to a large number of Mennonites. It was the one area in Ontario where they were able to buy several large tracts of land early in the nineteenth century. While this quilt has been well used, it has weathered exceedingly well.

This stunning Log Cabin Pineapple variation was made by an Armstrong relative in Peterborough County. The present owner remembers that this quilt was so special that it was kept in a trunk and seen only once a year, when his mother aired it. Fortunately, the Armstrongs have allowed it to be exhibited so that quilting students and admirers may study how important the scale of the logs and the placement of colour are to the overall design.

While this is a Scrap quilt, the quilter carefully placed her logs in each block. As you study a block you will notice that each corner position has the same fabric and that the centre squares of all the blocks are from the same piece of fabric. The blocks are about 13 inches square and each block has ten corner logs which create a large-diameter circular illusion. These blocks were sewn over a foundation during the quilt's construction, and the quilter chose not to add batting to the top. Instead, she backed it and then quilted "in the ditch" (in the seam line) through the three layers of fabric. As it was constructed with such care and obviously treasured by its creator, this quilt was possibly part of a trousseau. Whatever the reason for its making, it has been carefully maintained by succeeding generations.

Pineapple c. 1900
Peterborough County, Ontario
A member of the Armstrong family

Detail of Pineapple blocks

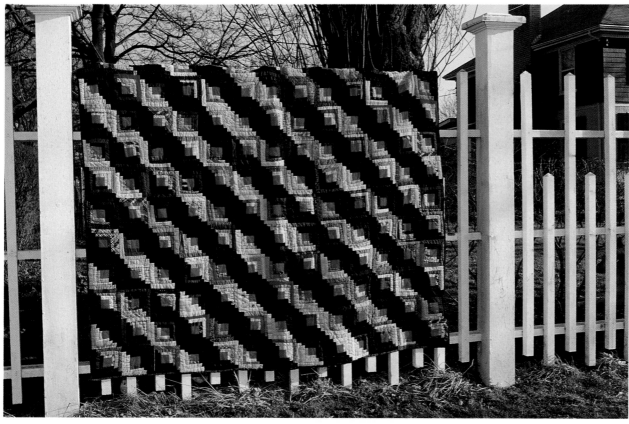

Straight Furrows c. 1895, Lutterworth Township, Ontario, Janet Robertson

This Straight Furrow Log Cabin quilt has been created from the usual suitings and flannelettes. The centres are also the usual red colour, and the blocks have been positioned in a "straight furrow" set, just as you would see in a well-ploughed field. Log Cabin quilts enabled Janet Robertson to use many small scrap pieces. When required, some of the logs were pieced on a diagonal so that the seaming was almost invisible.

Janet came from Scotland, where the winters were probably as cold and harsh as those in Ontario. This quilt has a woollen batting for extra warmth but still remains quite light in weight.

This silk-and-taffeta quilt was found in a family trunk when the Brinn family home in Tillsonburg was closed. Here we see an interesting dimensional appearance to the blocks, created by the placement of a light square at the centre of each block. Half of every block is black and arranged in such a manner as to give a strong diagonal line to the design, again a type of "straight furrow" set. The blocks were assembled and sewn over a foundation of muslin.

It is interesting to note that not all the centre squares are the same size, nor are all the blocks quite the same size. The result is that the quilt is not quite square. To the quilter of the day, however, this was not too important. The quilt was primarily made to be used, and because it was made from silks and taffetas, it was probably used for guests only.

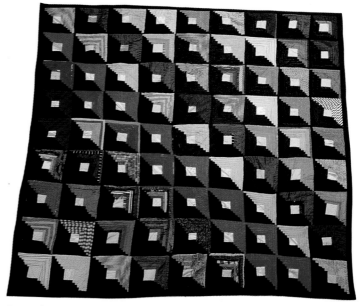

Straight Furrows c. 1900, Tillsonburg, Ontario

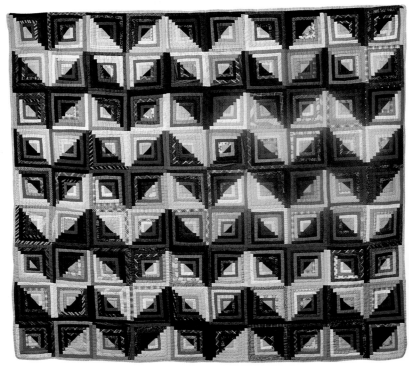

Chevron or **Zig Zag** c. 1900, Fenelon Falls, Ontario, Jennie Tiers

Jennie Tiers took great pride in her quilts. She made this particular winter quilt for her trousseau when she was 16 years old. She knew that every conscientious bride endeavoured to have ample bed linens for her forthcoming marriage. This Log Cabin quilt is made predominantly from woollen suitings and coatings, with cotton used for a few of the logs.

Note that Jennie divided the centre square in half so that the diagonal lines of her pattern would not be broken. Every centre contains the same orange-and-black fabric, which is the only constant in the top. The backing, which is also the binding, would have been purchased as woollen yard goods; Jennie must have wanted the additional warmth of a wool backing.

It takes a skilled quilter to quilt through the many thicknesses of such a design, and Jennie very skilfully quilted "in the ditch" (in the seam line) in every other log of each block. This quilt was meant to be used and it certainly was, since all the farmhouse bedrooms were unheated at the time.

The 1980s brought an explosion of new techniques, new tools and innovative methods of reworking traditional designs. The Log Cabin block, long a favourite with quilters, was one of the first blocks to be manipulated by comtemporary creative quilters.

Elsie Moser used an off-centre block to create an optical illusion of curves in her quilt. She sashed each of the blocks with black or off-white, depending on its location in the design. In order to further accentuate the curved illusion, Elsie quilted off-centre circles in each of the blocks and partial circles in the border.

In the background we see another pieced quilt with an interesting linear dimension. All the strips have been pieced with seam allowances to the front surface, and they are manipulated in the overall design to lie in opposing directions.

These quilts are displayed in a contemporary hall which blends traditional furnishings and upscale appointments.

Diamonds *c. 1898*
Ottawa Valley, Ontario

All the fabrics used in this Diamond set quilt are homespun and home-dyed fabrics. Farm women were very resourceful; they dyed their homespun fabrics using available plant materials such as beets for red, goldenrod or onion skins for yellow, and walnut shells for dark browns. Each family had its own recipes for dyeing fabrics, and these carefully guarded secrets were passed from one generation to the next.

This charming quilt from the Ottawa Valley reveals, in part, how a nineteenth-century family provided for all the necessities of home life. For instance, sheep were raised for their wool, which was then carded, dyed and woven into fabric. The linsey-woolsey scraps for this quilt were cuttings left over from the making of family clothes. The foundation for Scrap quilts was often cotton flannel, which helped make them extra warm for the severe winters.

Illusions *1985*
Ingersoll, Ontario
Elsie Moser

The clothing scraps used for quilting in the late 1800s were dark for winter and light for summer. The dyes for dark and light colours were generally stable, so these quilts are still very vibrant.

The colourful strips used in this Sunshine and Shadow quilt bring to mind many elements of nature: thin logs and thin branches as well as the traditional red for the hearth which kept the home fires burning. Here the red gives the quilt sparkle. It is little wonder that this design was such a favourite. No matter what fabric was used, the finished design was always appealing.

Sunshine and Shadow *c. 1900*
Louisville, Ontario

APPLIQUÉ QUILTS

The French word *appliqué* means applied, and it is used to denote both the technique and the decorative pieces used in it. Typically, the edges of the appliqué were carefully turned under to prevent fraying and then were sewn to the background fabric using tiny invisible slipstitches. With the resurgence of interest in quilting and appliqué which has been sweeping the country since the mid-1970s, this technique has also become more honed.

Broderie perse is a technique whereby elements from printed fabrics, chintzes or any other suitable fabrics are cut out and then appliquéd onto a plain ground fabric. These elements are usually applied using a very small buttonhole stitch or satin stitch, as the edges of the appliqué pieces are too detailed to be turned under.

It is possible that this technique was developed to achieve the look of stylish embroidery or crewel work which was very popular in Great Britain. It was also practised by a few of the settlers who immigrated to Canada from the U.S. as United Empire Loyalists. Many wonderful examples of broderie perse appear on Baltimore Album quilts found in public collections in the U.S. Sometimes embroidery was added to accent or complete a line or form part of a figure.

In order to create interesting appliqué, the quilter must have access to a variety of good-quality fabric scraps and have a well-developed sense of colour and design.

Flowers were very important to the farm wife and were frequently used on appliqué quilts. Mary Ann Reed was fortunate enough

Wreath of Wild Roses - Adaptation c. 1870, origin unknown, Mary Ann Reed

to have access to quality fabric when she chose to make this floral quilt. Here we see turkey red used for the petals; the green and orange fabric also had stable dyes. The orange centres were applied to the foundation first and then the red petal unit was applied and the centre cut out to allow the orange to show through. This is a simple form of reverse appliqué in which the stitcher cuts through one or more layers of fabric in order to create an illusion of depth. Mary Ann Reed must have felt more comfortable with this technique rather than having to

handle small orange circles which could be difficult to control.

Though Mary Ann was the mother of six children, she certainly must have had considerable free time for quilting, as she echoed the appliqué design in the large open areas and quilted it so tightly with her small stitches that she created a stipple effect in these areas. A simple curved line has been used within the appliqué unit, which serves to hold the layers of fabric together without detracting from the motif. This is a perfect example of quilting enhancing a design while

contributing to the longevity of the quilt. When cotton batting is quilted a quarter inch or closer, the batting is unable to migrate during laundering. Thus this quilt has kept its loft and is still in pristine condition. Since there is so much work in the quilt, it was probably made for a very special event such as a wedding.

Leaves are always colourful, whether lying on the ground in the fall or scattered across the surface of a quilt.

The quilt on the wall was made by Margaret (surname unknown), the great-great-aunt of the owner. Margaret lived in Chatham and enjoyed arranging and rearranging the leaves until she achieved a colour placement to her liking. The leaves were then connected with an embroidered vine that winds back and forth in each border. The soft green of the border and the soft pleasing shades of the leaves lift our spirits like a sunny spring day.

Edith Wilson was the wife of a United Church minister, and she often quilted with the women of Paris United Church. For this quilt she chose a wreath of apple blossoms, and many of the fabrics are similar to those used by Margaret. However, when you examine the yellow background fabric you can see that it did not all come from the same dye lot. Some of the yellow blocks are darker than others. Edith's vines have been appliquéd onto the background using bias strips of fabric. The large green triangles which form the first border give the quilt a springtime feel. However, this device was probably used for squaring-off the quilt, as the quilter had already run out of yellow fabric, save for an amount sufficient for the narrow outer border which is embellished with more leaves.

While both these women probably had large scrap bags, it is quite likely that they traded scraps with other quilters at quilting bees in order to increase the variety of prints available for their quilts.

In both these quilts, very simple quilting motifs have been used to enhance the designs. The diagonal grid has been combined with outline quilting by Edith, while Margaret chose a double-rope design.

Leaves and Vines *c. 1938, Chatham, Ontario, Margaret (surname unknown)*
Leaf Wreathes *1940, Paris, Ontario, Edith Wilson*

"Stuffed work" was not common among pioneer women, as it was time-consuming and did not wear well. Mary O'Grady was born in 1838 of Irish parents. Her father emigrated from Ireland and settled in Fallowfield, Ontario, where he worked on the Rideau Canal for his livelihood. Stuffed work was popular in Great Britain during much of the eighteenth century, and so it is possible that Mary's mother taught her the technique which she utilized in this quilt, her own special trousseau quilt.

Many quilters dyed their fabrics, and it is likely that the green fabric used in this quilt was home-dyed. It is now quite faded. Every element of the design has been heavily stuffed and tied to the back; all the floral elements have been heavily stuffed, as has the green serpentine border. In order to execute stuffed work, every design element has a slit made in the back in the foundation fabric, then the batting is stuffed in with a blunt tool until the desired pouf is achieved. Next, each of these slits are closed with a loose cross-stitch. This quilt was made as a summer quilt, with no batting, but the two layers of fabric have been quilted with a diagonal grid in the open areas.

One wonders where quilters get their inspirations for a technique. Did these gate bolts inspire this quilter?

Floral Trapunto c. 1860
Fallowfield, Ontario
Mary O'Grady

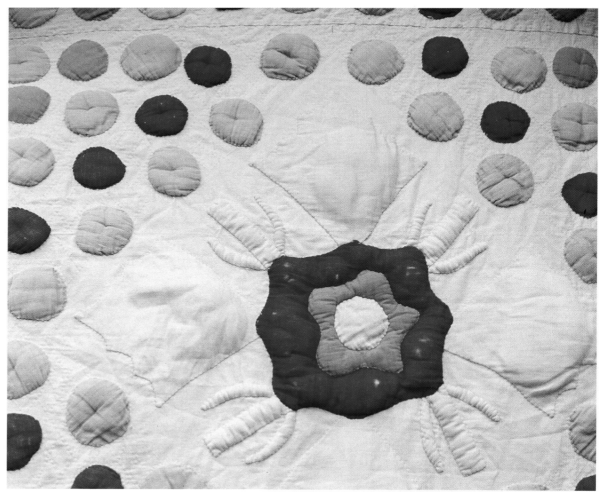

*Detail of **Floral Trapunto***
showing stuffed work

Armenia Devins appliquéd these blocks in 1911. While the present owner says the block was known as the Tree of Paradise pattern, it could also be called Forbidden Fruit. The fabrics used are typical of the colours available prior to World War I. As you examine many of the pre-1900 quilts, you will observe that the reds and oranges were very stable dyes, but not always so for the greens.

This top was not quilted until recently, when the present owner decided to add the picot points. It had been kept out of the light for 80 years and the fabrics still have the feel of new fabric. This is something quite unusual, as it is only in recent times that homes have had thermostats and humidity controls. The loft of the synthetic batting used, compounded by the fact that this quilt has never been laundered, prevents it from having the characteristic puckered charm of a laundered antique quilt.

Tree of Paradise c. 1911
Vaughn Township, Ontario
Armenia Devins

Pictorial Medallion 1827
origin unknown
Jane Reagan

Quilts tell a story and sometimes the content of the story depends upon the imagination of the viewer. This descriptive quilt was purchased in Ontario some 40 years ago and nothing is known about the quilter or origin of the quilt. However, upon careful examination it is immediately obvious that the quilter understood the technique of broderie perse.

The focal point of this quilt top is the centre area where the chintz has been cut and appliquéd with no apparent thought to the subject matter or the elements surrounding it. Jane Reagan tells her life story through the medium of fabric and thread. Great care has been taken in cutting the design elements from an assortment of cotton fabrics. Since the top is not completed, we might assume that the quilter died before it was finished, but one may wonder whether the artist died young or old. The more you examine this top, the more you realize the hundreds of hours of work put into drawing the basic templates and then spent cutting the fabrics. Special attention was given to positioning the templates on the fabrics, as the quilter hoped to achieve a feeling of realism.

Details of 1827 Pictorial Medallion

It is likely that this signed and dated Memory quilt was inspired by the harsh Canadian environment, a sharp contrast to the surroundings in which the quilter was raised in the Old Country. The upper three-quarters of the quilt tell of life before she arrived in Canada. For instance, this young woman was courted in an arbour. Note that the young couple was chaperoned. It appears life was wonderful and the quilter's dreams were many!

The quilter was a talented artist and able to effectively silhouette both human and animal shapes from her fabric scraps.

The two sides of this quilt probably depict memory scenes from youth: dancing, being entertained by jesters, going to church, visiting, travelling and participating in castle life. Perhaps this was where the quilter once lived herself. Across the top we see elements from her childhood home. The figures were probably meant to represent her own family members. The print chosen for the needlewoman provides a curvaceous female shape, which can also be observed in the other woman. Observe the detail— many pictures on the wall above the mantel, flowers on one table and scissors on another. The castle was cut from a single piece of fabric and needled skilfully onto the foundation. Jane probably had a wonderful memory and was quite fastidious in recording her memories.

*Details of 1827 **Pictorial Medallion** showing date and skilful use of fabric scraps*

*Detail showing log cabin, shamrock and fiddle in the **Pictorial Medallion** quilt*

The final chapter—Jane's life in the New World—is depicted across the bottom of the quilt. She probably arrived as a bride, full of hopes and dreams. Her home was a log cabin, perhaps built on Crown land. Farming was the couple's source of livelihood. She depicts herself here tilling the ground with crude tools presumably made by her husband.

If a picture is worth a thousand words, this exquisite pictorial quilt tells us of a lifetime. The top was probably started before 1827 and some of the fabrics would predate this. Jane probably brought the fabrics and threads with her when she came to Canada. Imported fabrics and threads of this quality were not available in remote areas. Several pieces of fabric still bear the Royal Seal of Approval on their backs. Fabrics had to be of top quality before they were given this approval.

Observe how Jane positioned her cabin template on the fabric to achieve the structural effect of a log cabin. She also has a shamrock and a fiddle beside the cabin, symbols that make one speculate that she came from Ireland.

Unfortunately, this quilt has not had the best of care and is presently in an advanced state of rot. It will not be available for future generations to admire, but fortunately it has been photographed for our enjoyment.

Jane must have been very proud of her work. This quilt is signed and dated 1827 and tells quite a story. However, there are no children in the tale. One wonders if Jane's dreams for a long and happy life were realized during a time when many unfortunate women succumbed to the complications of childbirth.

This charming appliqué quilt was made in the Toronto area circa 1920. The foundation for the design is intersecting circles which are embellished with a floral motif. The quilter definitely added an element of interest to the floral treatment by using two shades of rose for the petals and two shades of green for the leaves. The construction is a block method in which the stem curves in from corner to corner around the four sides of the block. A flower is then applied to the intersection as well as in the middle of the curve. The leaves are spaced between the flowers. The design is outline-quilted and a simple floral motif has been used in the open areas.

The quilter was an accomplished sewer; there is a scalloped edge to the quilt which has been carefully bound with bias-cut fabric which matches that used in the quilt. The border treatment echoes the central motif and creates an interesting appliquéd drop for the side of the bed.

This quilt was made for a doctor by his secretary, and one can only assume that it was for a very special event, since it was made with such great care.

Wedding Rose *c. 1920*
Toronto, Ontario

Flowers can be enjoyed at any time of the year. Rose of Sharon is one of the few bushes that comes into full bloom in midsummer. Anna Henderson wanted to capture the spirit of summer in this appliquéd quilt—memories of sunny summer days spent lounging in the shade of a large Rose of Sharon bush. Perhaps she was recollecting the Jerseyville area where her family were some of the first settlers.

Anna was meticulous with her appliqué. She cut out all the foundation fabric from behind each flower, so there was no shadowing through of colours as one fabric was layered on top of another in the construction of the flowers. The fabrics chosen provide a pleasant blend of colour, much like the shades of the flower itself. To complete her quilt, Anna outline-quilted the motifs and then quilted floral units in the large open areas.

Rose of Sharon *c. 1930*
Lynden, Ontario
Anna Henderson

Daffodil Wreath c. 1880, Durham, Ontario, Annie Branchflower Allin

Winter months allowed a quilter many relaxing hours for piecing and quilting. During the darkest months of the year Annie Allin's thoughts probably turned to spring, as she chose a sunny yellow fabric to create this attractive floral wreath quilt.

All the motifs have been embroidered to the foundation block with a stem stitch which gives a crisp edge to the appliqué. The floral motif was outline-quilted and simple leaves were quilted in the sashing. This cheery quilt was probably for spring and summer use in the Allin household. Upon her death, Annie left a legacy of quilts for her relatives to treasure and enjoy.

Blossoms and flowers have always been a source of inspiration for quilters. Mrs. C.A. Arnold enjoyed the relaxation of creating quilts without the stress of designing them. She was born in 1892 and lived in St. Thomas, Ontario.

This U.S. kit quilt was done in the 1940s. During her long, productive life Mrs. Arnold made many quilts which are still enjoyed by her family members.

Handsewing was this quilter's specialty, and this charming quilt has been completely hand-appliquéd and exquisitely quilted utilizing several variations of the feathered-wreath motif. This quilt was made for a bed without a footboard, as the corners have been carefully appliquéd and the open areas quilted extensively.

Rose Wreath c. 1945, St. Thomas, Ontario, Mrs. C.A. Arnold

This was a beautiful quilt made by Bridget McNamara Henesy for her trousseau. It was her favourite of many quilts and was used only on special occasions. Unfortunately, after her death, this treasure fell into the hands of owners who did not give it much care. It was used and laundered with harsh detergents which faded the colours drastically. The green has changed the most, from its original dark shade to its present pale hue. The red and yellow were once much brighter also.

Bridget created this quilt with almost invisible appliqué stitches. She used red quilting thread in the floral areas where she quilted double rows of stitches. All of the quilting was executed with double rows of small uniform stitches, which give a wonderful texture to the surface of this special quilt.

Laura Ashenhurst's parents subscribed to the *Family Herald* magazine, a farm publication in the early 1900s. Since she lived in the rural community of Apsley, Laura obtained her printed fabrics by ordering half-yard pieces from the Eaton's and Simpsons catalogues. The pattern for this quilt was traced from the *Family Herald*. Laura appliquéd the blocks in the evening by lamplight. During the Christmas holidays she was assisted with the quilting by her sisters Olla and Greta, her Aunt Ethel and a neighbour friend. These women kept the quilting very simple, just following the outline of the pattern.

The quilt gives you the feeling of looking into a flower. The middle of the central unit was cut out and turned under rather than appliquéing another piece on top. This enabled the foundation fabric for the block to serve as the centre of each floral unit.

Rose Wreath c. 1890
Ingersoll, Ontario
Bridget McNamara Henesy

Rose of Sharon Variation 1935
Apsley, Ontario
Laura Ashenhurst

Noonday Sun *or* ***Rising Sun*** *c. 1860*
County Tyrone, Ireland

This graphic appliqué floral design is known as Noonday Sun or Rising Sun. It was made in Tyrone County, Ireland, in 1860 and was brought to Canada by Gladys Grass when she immigrated here late in the nineteenth century.

Handsewing was greatly enjoyed by Irish gentry. Upon careful observation, you can see that all the yellow petals on the inner ring have been gathered in order to give dimension and a little more realism to the floral units. Orange was a popular colour at the time. This quilt was both carefully handpieced and appliquéd. Used as a bedcovering for most of its life, it now adorns a table until such time as dinner is served.

When these quilts were made, the motor car had not yet been invented and the horse and carriage was the mode of transportation used for visiting.

Colonial Lady was a popular pattern shared by many quilters. The quilters could be as elaborate as their scrap bags and imaginations allowed. Alice Touchburn made the quilt in the carriage as a gift for her son and his new wife. It was used and enjoyed by them for many years, but some of the fabric is now rotting away.

Highways and expressways did not exist in the 1920s. Roads were narrow and winding, as they often followed Indian trails or stream beds. The pattern of the quilt in the carriage is known as Drunkard's Path—it winds its way back and forth across the surface of the quilt, mimicking the path of a staggering drunkard. This is a two-colour design which afforded Christinea Lillian Copperthwaite an opportunity to purchase a piece of fabric to make this top rather than having to make the quilt from her scrap bag.

Drunkard's Path c. 1920
Dartford, Ontario
Christinea Lillian Copperthwaite
Colonial Lady c. 1910
Bethany, Ontario
Alice Touchburn

Colonial Lady c. 1930, Sydney, Nova Scotia, Myrtle Bonnyman

Sunbonnet Lady c. 1940, Dunnville, Ontario, Mabel Calvert

Quilt kits were popular during the 1930s, when not all quilters had access to inventories of scrap fabrics. Myrtle Bonnyman lived in Sydney, Nova Scotia, and enjoyed embroidering, probably more than quilting. She carefully positioned the ladies on the block and affixed them with a uniform buttonhole stitch done in thread to match the appliqué. The design has been completed with an assortment of stitches, such as stem, running, satin and French knots. This kit probably came complete with embroidery floss, as the threads are a perfect match for each block. The advantage of a kit was that the purchaser did not need to procure additional supplies.

These blocks did not come with sashing or backing fabric, so Myrtle chose a blending white cotton for this purpose. It appears she decided to make a summer quilt and used flannelette for the batting, which gives some warmth with little loft. The quilting has been kept to a minimum. There is only a double row of outline quilting around the appliqué (echo quilting), and simple cross-hatching in the sashing and border areas.

Colonial Lady remained a popular design during the 1930s and 1940s, when quilting was again done out of necessity. During World War II, fabrics and money were scarce. Many of the

men were off fighting the war, and there was always the anxiety of whether or not they would return home alive. The scrap bag became a very important item in the family household. All women and girls were encouraged to develop their needle skills. Myrtle Bonnyman searched her scrap bag for bright prints for this quilt. She embellished the hats and umbrellas with embroidery, as well as outlining the arms. Myrtle accentuated the figures with a stem stitch around the outside edge of all the appliquéd units.

While the 1930s were dark times economically, the 1940s were stressful years emotionally. Quilters enjoyed dreaming and fantasizing about exciting bygone eras. This colourful quilt is shown at the elegant Queenston, Ontario, home of William Lyon Mackenzie, founder of the *Colonial Advocate* newspaper in 1824, a very popular newspaper in Upper Canada. Here one can conjure up thoughts of beautiful ladies socializing in elegant surroundings.

Sunbonnet Sue and Brother Bill *c. 1930*
Tillsonburg, Ontario
Alice Chandler

Sunbonnet Sue Variation *1971*
Georgetown, Ontario
Helen Archer

All members of the Chandler family had their own quilts, and here at the Ball home we see a 1930 Sunbonnet Sue quilt made for a young daughter. Life was difficult during the Depression, when Alice Chandler wanted to make a special quilt for her daughter. In order not to use any additional thread in appliquéing the motifs, she embroidered the blocks to the background with black embroidery floss. Additional embroidery was then used to embellish the motifs.

Many farm newspapers printed a quilting block in their weekly editions, and it is quite likely that Alice got these two blocks from such a source.

In order to make this a durable quilt, flannelette sheeting was used for batting, the front and back were pieced from factory cotton, and the back was made of coarser, less-expensive fabric. Alice pieced and quilted this everyday child's quilt on her treadle sewing machine. The quilting is sparse, only around the blocks, as it was not necessary to quilt sheeting to stop the migration of batting during laundry.

This child's quilt is displayed on a youth's bed with a treasured doll which has also been much loved and enjoyed by its owner.

Everybody loves a baby, and Helen Archer, a friend of Alice's grandmother, made this quilt as a gift when Alice was born.

A sense of femininity has been achieved through the careful choice of fabric scraps. The apron fabric is a lightweight cotton which allows the skirt fabric to shadow through, much like it would in reality. A touch of lace and embroidery plus simple quilting complete the design of this delicate, whimsical quilt made for a special granddaughter. It is seen here cascading from the drawer of a child's dresser in the Ball home in Jordan.

Log Cabin c. 1940 *(chair)*
Douro, Ontario
Mary Whibbs
Appliqué *c. 1860*
Fenelon Falls, Ontario
Mrs. Simpson
Hexagon *c. 1900*
Paola, Indiana

What could be more beautiful for Christmas? In the master bedroom of this authentically restored 1830 home in Niagara-on-the-Lake, we see a masterfully appliquéd quilt (c. 1860) with an assortment of motifs. The cherries in the fruit bowl have all been stuffed to give added dimension.

Paper-cutting was common, as it was the easiest way of creating shapes for appliqué. The yellow double hearts as well as the stylized leaf and acorn motifs would have been created by folding paper several times and then cutting out the drawn design. In this case the designs were drawn quartered; that is, a piece of paper was folded into quarters. Some quilters first drew a basic design

and then cut it out—it was always a surprise to see what shape would emerge when the paper was opened up. Quilters in the 1800s had few patterns, so folded-paper art was an easy and available method of creating original motifs.

Mrs. Simpson was an experienced needlewoman, as her appliqué stitches are almost invisible. The surface of the quilt was heavily quilted, with very small stitches outlining the motifs. Unfortunately, not all the dyes were stable and the green has faded badly. Otherwise, the quilt is still in excellent condition.

Little is known about the graphic Hexagon quilt (c. 1900) lying on the blanket box except

that it came from Indiana. It is a wonderful example of the resourcefulness of the quilter. The quilt was perfectly pieced using colours of fabric common at the time. This quilter ran out of orange fabric, hence some of the hexagons at the bottom of the quilt were painted. Unfortunately, the paint hardened, so this area of the quilt has been given special care over the years to prevent the fibres from breaking down.

When room did not permit a quilt rack in the corner, quilts were folded and piled on a chair or bench. On the stencilled chair rests a Log Cabin quilt created by Mary Whibbs. Mary used her scraps carefully to create a quilt which makes a perfect comple-

ment to this Christmas setting. It is interesting that she chose the same colour for the centres of her logs as for the logs themselves. This makes the furrows very pronounced, since there is no accent.

The hooked carpet on the floor complements the quilts in the room. This carpet was made in eastern Ontario or in Chéticamp, New Brunswick. While the fireplace could heat the room, the wooden floors were never warm. A hooked carpet was a welcome addition to any bedroom, as was the bedwarmer leaning in the corner, just waiting to be used.

Detail of appliqué work and quilting on Mrs. Simpson's quilt shown opposite

PAPER CUT OR HAWAIIAN

Paper-cutting was an interesting technique practised by nineteenth-century European needlers and perfected by the Hawaiians during the twentieth century.

The pioneer housewife had few tools other than a pencil and scissors with which to design her quilts. She did, however, have a supply of used newspapers, old brown waxed paper and cardboard which she could fold and cut into interesting shapes to use as pattern pieces for an appliqué quilt.

Designs usually took the form of a single, large, stylized appliqué cut freehand from a large piece of cloth folded into quarters or eighths. The appliqué was placed in the centre of the quilt and sometimes bordered. Echo quilting, or quilting which follows the outline of the appliqué, was often used to give an undulating effect to the quilt's surface, similar to a pebble skipping across the water's surface.

Paper-cutting was used well into the 1970s as a means of making shapes which were used for quilting designs. Many of the quilting designs were very simple shapes, such as exotic tropical plant leaves or pumpkin seeds. These shapes were cut from old letters, envelopes, cardboard, tin—anything available in the home. Often a husband would make a tin template for his wife for a special quilting motif which she would use on many quilts.

The paper-cutting technique was taught to the Hawaiians by missionaries. They have expanded and honed it to such a high degree of sophistication that most paper-cut appliqué is now referred to as Hawaiian!

Paper Cut c. 1885, Williamsburg, Ontario, Phoebe Garlough McIntosh

Paper-cut designs were easy for a quilter to copy. This was done by folding a piece of suitably sized paper into quarters and then tracing one quarter of the design along the folded edge. The fabric was folded in the same manner. Next, the quilter traced around the pattern which was placed on the folded fabric. When the fabric was cut with scissors and opened out, this produced a full design.

Phoebe Garlough McIntosh, the grandmother of the present owner, made this quilt as part of her trousseau. It was intended as a summer quilt, since it has no batting. Hence, Phoebe was able to keep her quilting stitches minute and very even—an indication of a skilled quilter, even at the young age of 20.

The shade of orange she used was common during the mid to late 1800s, and we have to wonder whether Phoebe dyed her fabric or purchased it already dyed. Young women enjoyed making Appliqué quilts for their trousseaus, as it afforded them an opportunity to show their sewing skills. It was important that a woman be proficient at sewing, as she was expected to provide her family with all their clothes and linens. Pheobe certainly had extensive practise as a young girl; her appliqué stitches are so small as to be almost invisible.

Annie Reed was born in Wellington County in 1865. She was of Scottish background and this Scottish Thistle quilt bespeaks her heritage. The six large units were probably designed by the folding and paper-cutting technique, while the other elements were probably drawn on paper or cardboard and then traced onto the fabric. The clamshell quilting design was commonly used, since it required only the first line to be drawn, then the quilter could "eyeball" successive lines.

The border design creates the effect of leaves and branches blowing in the wind and extends the central motif onto the sides of the antique rope bed, which was common in early Ontario.

Some families were fortunate to have hooked rugs surrounding their beds, as the floors were always cold. These antique carpets echo the thistle and patchwork motifs so prevalent in nineteenth-century Ontario.

Scottish Thistles c. 1890
Wellington County, Ontario
Annie Reed

Here we see a signed and dated 1858 quilt which exhibits the smallest of appliqué stitches on its totally handworked surface. For added interest Jane Snider appliquéd a serpentine vine-and-leaf border around her central oak leaf motif. For a quilting design Jane used a trailing leaf throughout the open area. While it is not known for certain that Jane made the linen fringe, one assumes she did, since it has been as precisely worked as the appliqué and the quilting design. If she did make it, it is likely that she had a supply of linen yarn on hand, as cotton was very difficult to procure at the time. (Cotton yarn was imported from the United States, which was in a state of upheaval due to the Civil War.) Once again, we see the use of the popular turkey red, which, together with the fringe, has withstood the tests of wear and time.

Oak Leaf *1858*
Owen Sound, Ontario
Jane Snider

*Detail of **Oak Leaf** pattern*

Red and white has long been a favourite colour combination for quilters. By placing a bright red-and-white quilt on white-painted furniture, a woman could easily change her decorating scheme from winter to summer.

Sarah Sproule had a collection of embroidery designs which she assembled into a quilt. As the designs are all simple and youthful, the quilt was probably made for a child. No effort was made to embellish the embroidery blocks.

Here are two appliqué quilts made using paper-cutting techniques. Both were made as a learning experience. Mrs. Adam Underwood made the Medallion quilt and perfected her appliqué stitches; they are almost invisible. This quilt was included in her personal effects when she immigrated to Canada in 1909. Ada Balls, assisted by her mother, made her version of the Wedding Tulip in 1904. She had clearly learned many of the intricacies of quilting when she made this quilt for her hope chest. The lining and backing were made from bleached flour sacks, while all the new fabric was used for the design side. The quilting on both these quilts is sparse but well planned.

The butterflies were appliquéd onto separate blocks and four blocks were seamed together for this quilt design. All appliqué has been executed with a buttonhole stitch using embroidery floss in shades of green and black. The cotton for the blocks is coarse and the border fabric is bleached sugar bags. It is interesting to note that the backing is a good-quality muslin.

Quilters love to reproduce scenes from nature, and butterfly quilts were popular in the 1930s and 1940s. This special quilt now shows some evidence of wear, as the embroidery stitches are breaking and coming loose. Rows of chaining have been quilted the length of this fanciful quilt for texture and loft.

Embroidered Sampler c. 1893, Cannington, Ontario, Sarah Sproule; **Leaves (Medallion)** c. 1900, England, Mrs. Adam Underwood; **Wedding Tulip** 1904, Woodstock, Ontario, Ada Balls

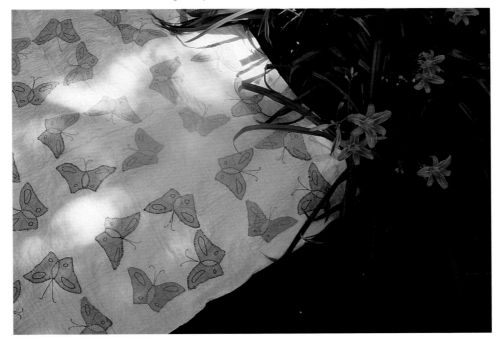

Embroidered-appliquéd Butterflies c. 1930, Stouffville, Ontario

Celtic Appliqué *c. 1850*
Acton, Ontario
Jane Graham Hill
Tulip *c. 1883*
Ridgetown, Ontario
Amelia Eskritt

On the bed we see a lightweight summer quilt which has very thin batting. In some places you can see what appear to be cotton seeds. While the quilt, at first glance, seems to have been made using a Celtic design technique, it was actually constructed from paper-cut units appliquéd to the white background. Jane Graham Hill (1827-1906) appliquéd her design elements with a tiny overcast stitch.

Jane must have enjoyed quilting, as all the open areas have been worked with leaf and floral motifs and all the design elements have been outline-quilted one-

quarter of an inch from the edges. For additional interest Jane included a decorative edge of half ovals, which she first finished with a bias edge. While little is known about why this quilt was made, it may be assumed that it was a wedding quilt. It was a time-consuming piece of work that was executed with much care and pride.

Draped over the foot-rail is another appliquéd tulip variation. Unfortunately, as the fabric is layered, it is the top appliqué layer that gets the most wear and therefore deteriorates first. Like all young women of her era, Amelia

Eskritt made a number of quilts for her hope chest. In 1883 she married Brewin Roadhouse, and she lived in Essex County until her death in 1948.

Amelia scaled down the central pattern and created a complementary border design to frame the central four-block medallion design. She quilted a clamshell design across the surface of the quilt, which gives texture without creating a secondary design.

COMMEMORATIVE & PATRIOTIC QUILTS

Autograph *1930*
Ingersoll, Ontario
Women's Auxiliary of Trinity United Church

During the nineteenth century, special textiles were manufactured to celebrate a variety of events: a coronation, a royal visit, a political occasion, sporting activity or historical event. Pieces of such fabrics, along with printed ribbons and handkerchiefs, were collected and pieced into quilts.

Church groups often raised money by selling church members the opportunity to have their signatures on a quilt, with the cost per signature ranging from 10 to 25 cents. These quilts usually bear a date and serve as an excellent record of church membership at a given time. A commemorative quilt was often made by the church women as a gift for a retiring minister, who was always a grateful recipient.

The Women's Auxiliary of Trinity United Church in Ingersoll designed and quilted this autograph quilt to record the names of church members and ministers who were active in the presbytery during the early 1930s. In order to raise money for their church they solicited the congregation, and for the princely sum of 10 cents a member's name would be embroidered on the quilt.

A six-pointed star was chosen for the embroidery motif and was executed using a stem stitch and mauve embroidery floss. The pattern allowed a total of 23 names to be included on each block. Many of the blocks include several family members, and some blocks are all family members. If you look carefully at the third block from the left in the second row down, you will see the name Mitch Hepburn, the Premier of Ontario from 1934 to 1942.

The quilters of Trinity United Church were also interested in preserving the image of their church as it was at the time. Thus they embroidered a replica of the building in the centre of this quilt. The names of the women involved in the design and quilting are among the many parishioners chronicled in this visual record of a church's membership.

The Hattie Johnston Missionary Society co-ordinated the making of the blocks for this quilt. Each block was made by a different African Methodist Church group in Ontario. Each church group charged 10 cents to individuals who wished to have their name put on a block. Every church is identified, since each group embroidered its name around the central area, which has been worked with French knots. The completed blocks were returned to the town of Harrow, where the women of the Hattie Johnston Missionary Society sashed the blocks and completed the quilt. Unfortunately, they chose not to quilt the top, so with years of handling the batting has wadded and migrated into lumps in an area of each block.

This quilt is a wonderful record of Blacks in Ontario at the turn of the century, most of whom were directly descended from slaves who fled to Canada during the 1800s. These slaves started arriving after 1812, when Canada declared Black residents to be free people. For the next 60 years they arrived via the Underground Railroad. While there are no accurate figures, it has been estimated that by 1860 some 30,000 Blacks had arrived in Ontario. They were clustered in numerous communities along the shores of Lake Erie and along a route from Niagara Falls west to Amherstburg, the route of the Underground Railroad.

Amherstburg was very accessible to fleeing slaves. Situated at the narrowest point of the Detroit River, it was a prime location for slaves fleeing the United States to be ferried across by boat. In the winter, when the ice on the river was firm, they would walk across. Those that came via the Underground Railroad were led by brave leaders such as Harriet Tubman, who escorted these

A.M.E. Conference Quilt 1925, Harrow, Ontario, Hattie Johnston Missionary Society

desperate people at night as they made their way north. Fleeing the United States was dangerous. Anyone caught was likely to be put to death. Angry owners often sent spies to look for their fleeing slaves. As time progressed, communities were formed inland in dense bush areas. This made it more difficult to track those who

had escaped.

It is interesting to study the names of the groups who contributed to this quilt. They were Canaan MMS, Grand MMS, Toronto, Oakville Missionary Lurner Chapel, Chatham, Sarnia, Hamilton, Amherstburg Central Grove. Note that the Hamilton group used gold thread for its

French knots. One can only speculate that they were unable to procure the same embroidery thread as that used by all the other groups.

Quilts were a wonderful way to record membership in congregations during a time when life was difficult and records were not always kept.

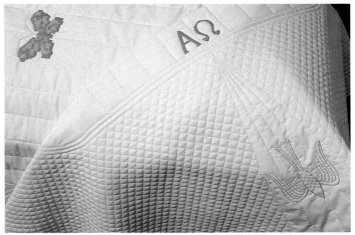

*Detail of **Embroidered Pall** showing quilting and embroidery*

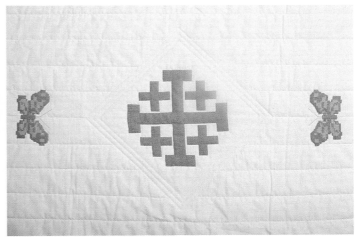

Detail showing the embroidered Jerusalem Cross

Embroidered Pall 1991
Niagara-on-the-Lake, Ontario
Niagara Sew and Sewers

The use of palls dates back to 1425, when history records their use in the early Roman Catholic Church. The tradition was maintained in the Anglican Church. Usually, the pall was owned by the church and was made of black, purple or white velvet. Here is a modern reproduction which was created to replace a much worn and undersized antique one. Church vestments have historically exhibited fine needlework, and the five Niagara-on-the-Lake women known as the Sew and Sewers, who combined their talents to create this contemporary pall, needled the religious symbols in fine gold thread and then crosshatched the surface for simple beauty.

In the centre we see the Jerusalem Cross, which is composed of five crosses representing the five wounds of Jesus. On either side of the cross is a butterfly, a religious symbol of the resurrection. The doves in the corners symbolize the Holy Spirit, and alpha and omega are Greek letters signifying the beginning and the end.

Some traditions carry on, and thanks to these talented quilters, St. Marks Church in Niagara-on-the-Lake will possess this beautiful pall for many years to come.

In 1943 Edna Climenhage's husband, Albert, was very ill. While attending to his personal needs 24 hours a day, she learned that her only son had been killed in World War II. To cope with her grief, Edna started this quilt, which was perfectly handpieced using only knitted woollens—army underwear and socks, the only personal effects of her son that were returned to her. These woollens were very difficult to sew once they had been cut. While she had sufficient underwear, Edna had to augment the socks with socks that had been left at home. Hence, this grieving woman was able to construct a beautiful quilt in memory of her son and simultaneously save the only tangible articles worn by him up until his untimely death.

Sadly, grief for this quilter was twofold. Shortly after her son was killed, Edna's husband also died. Upon completion of the quilt immortalizing her son, she embarked upon another quilt utilizing neckties belonging to her husband and son. What a thoughtful way to preserve personal apparel and important memories for oneself and for the succeeding generations who would never have the opportunity to know these two special gentlemen. Since Albert was the local undertaker, it seemed appropriate that the quilt be displayed resting on a pew in the local funeral home.

This design is created entirely of diamond-shaped pieces of silky fabrics. It is assembled with a random colour placement. The optical outcome is quite ambiguous and the eye tends to focus more on the luminous effect created by the fabrics. If you look carefully, it is possible to see some six-pointed stars.

Friendship Circle 1943
Stevensville, Ontario
Edna Climenhage

Glory Block 1945, *Stevensville, Ontario, Edna Climenhage*

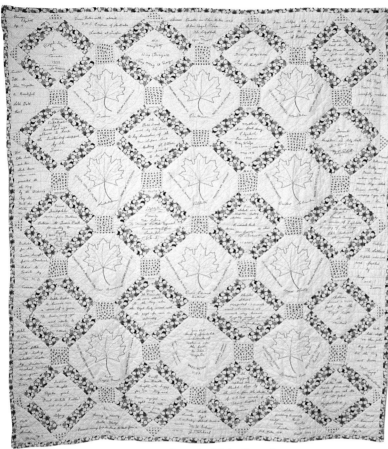

The Royal Visit 1939, Toronto, Ontario, Violet Laccohee

Stuart composed the tune "Soldiers of the Queen" as a memorial for the soldiers who fought in the Boer War (1899-1902). The quilter is unknown, but she used the Dresden Plate block and her scraps to create a Medallion quilt. The border has been constructed as a Crazy quilt with a partial Dresden Plate motif in each corner.

Upon inspection you can see the embroidered inscription: "Best wishes Ida." Perhaps Ida made this top and gave it to a friend to quilt; however, it was never completed.

This patriotic top was photographed on the wall of a lookout tower at Fort George in Niagara-on-the-Lake. Two rifles from the War of 1812 rest against it. Niagara-on-the-Lake was the first capital of Upper Canada. It was saved from American in-

vaders through the combined efforts of British regulars and Canadian militia under the leadership of General Sir Isaac Brock.

Soldiers of the Queen
by Leslie Stuart

*It's the soldiers of the Queen,
my lads
Who've been my lads,
Who're seen my lads
In the fight for England's
glory, lads,
When we've had to show them
what we mean
And when we say we've always won,
And when they ask us
how it's done,
We'll proudly point to every one of
England's soldiers of the Queen
It's the Queen*

Commemorative quilts are made for many reasons. Violet Laccohee made this quilt for her daughter, Mary Lou, who was nine at the time of the Royal visit in 1939. Her daughter wanted to remember everything about the King and Queen coming to Canada.

There are 12 maple leaf blocks which represent the journey. Nine stand for the provinces in the order in which they were visited. The other three are dedicated to the Royal Canadian Mounted Police Guard of Honour during the tour, Mrs. Roosevelt (who supplied her signature), and the Canadian Press. The sashing for the blocks denotes the decorations and maple leaves of all the cities, while the small print at the intersections represents all the towns

and villages that the King and Queen did not see. All the signatures were collected by Violet, except those of the King and Queen and Lord Tweedsmuir, which were taken from reproductions in newspapers. Along the bottom of the quilt is a small family record of significant events.

Surprisingly, it only took seven months to collect the signatures and complete the quilt. Mary Lou has a wonderful memento of the Royal visit in this lovingly executed quilt by her now deceased mother.

Panels and scraps are a favourite way of preserving treasured memories. The maker who creatively assembled this top definitely had ties to Britain, and many fond memories. Leslie

Scrap Fan Medallion Variation c. 1920, Weston, Ontario

Opercula I and II 1976, Ottawa, Ontario, Dorothea Powell

Quilting is a method of recording history. Here we have two quilts created in 1976 upon the owner's return from a diplomatic posting in England. Using standard brass-rubbing techniques, the designs were rubbed from coal covers found in the immediate vicinity of a London house built in the 1800s. These cast-iron covers were either solid, ventilated or illuminated (with solid-glass inserts). When coal was delivered, the coal heaver would remove the lid and pour the coal straight into the coal bin below ground. Entry to the coal bin was from the basement of the house.

The quilter, Dorothea Powell, had her rubbings photographed when she returned to Canada. She placed the photographs in an epidiascope to enlarge the design to a suitable size and then traced them onto tracing paper. Next, the designs were filled in, using fabric crayon on the back of the tracing. Finally, using a hot iron, these designs were transferred onto a neutral tergal fabric.

If you look carefully you can read some of the inscriptions on the coal covers: G. Guy Orchard St. W, A. Smellie & Co. Ltd. Westminster SW1, Hayward Brothers Self Fastening Coal Plate, Addis's Ventilating Grate, Charle's Safety Plate. The squares were quilted following the designs, then sewn together and bordered. Here we see the fronts and backs of two quilts created from the quilter's numerous rubbings. They are being watched over by an antique china doll.

Shawls were a part of every British woman's wardrobe until the middle of the twentieth century. When the Linklaters sailed from the Orkney Islands off the coast of Scotland in 1852, Mrs. Margaret Linklater brought with her this paisley shawl. It was probably woven in the town of Paisley, Scotland, where a Mr. Paterson had established a weaving mill in the early 1800s. It took approximately one week to weave a shawl such as this. The Linklaters' voyage took 17 weeks.

Upon arriving in Canada, the family made its way to York, where Margaret Laura Linklater was born two weeks later. Bedding was scarce in the New World, so Margaret's soft, warm shawl was used to wrap the new baby. It was subsequently used as the family receiving blanket and it bundled many more of the Linklater bairns.

Eventually, Margaret decided to preserve this shawl by making it into a quilt. Here it rests over the back of a chair while two antique dolls nestle in its luxurious folds of fine wool.

Wool is easy to quilt. Feather and feather-wreath motifs have been used in the central area to complement the cone or seed-pod design (a symbol of life and fertility) on the border of the shawl.

Houses are warmer now, but this shawl could still be draped around the shoulders of one of today's family members on a chilly winter evening.

Paisley Shawl c. 1900
Markham Township, Ontario
Margaret Laura (Linklater) Quantz

Red, white and blue are three favourite quilting colours. For Canadians, the colours are part of their heritage—the Union Jack combines these colours, and military uniforms were red and white—so we photographed these quilts in the barracks at Fort George in Niagara-on-the-Lake. Red and blue dyes were two of the first dyes to be made colourfast. Turkey red was perfected in the eighteenth century and indigo blue dates back to the sixteenth century.

In the foreground we see a simple Nine-patch, probably created from scrap shirting and sashed with red-and-white-sprigged muslin. A simple quilt such as this would often be used on a child's bed, as it is colourful and quickly constructed.

Feathered Stars were usually made for special occasions. This one, handpieced by Mrs. Robert McBride using a navy microdot, was probably made during the late 1800s as a wedding gift for a relative who subsequently immigrated to Canada.

The Pinwheel variation conjures up an image of schoolchildren waving flags at a parade. The quilter was probably of British extraction and enjoyed working with these three patriotic colours. The quilt has been constructed from four large blocks which are sashed and centred with a blue pinwheel. While this is a graphic handpieced quilt, the piecing is not as precise as it could have been. One might surmise that it was made as a bed quilt for a child who favoured these patriotic colours, since it is simply quilted with straight lines.

Hanging on the wall is a well-worn Hole-in-the-Barn-Door quilt. Quilts were made to be used, and this one has been used and enjoyed by several generations of Hicklings, who have been farmers in the Barrie area since they

homesteaded there in the mid-1800s. Minnie was a prolific quilter during her lifetime. When the quilts became worn, she replaced them with new ones and gave the worn ones to the hired hand for his bed. This one was retrieved from there by her daughter-in-law, Muriel. It was made by Minnie herself, who was born in 1864. She owned a sewing machine by the time she made this entirely machine-pieced quilt. The

small striped sashing is a perfect accent to the black and white blocks. The fabric is probably shirting and dress scraps of white and red prints. The clamshell quilting design gives an ethereal undulation to the surface when it is viewed on the vertical plane.

Resting on the bench is a hand-pieced Pinwheel Scrap quilt (c. 1920). It possibly came from an eastern Ontario farm home where the fabric scrap bag was running

low. Like the quilt above, this one was also meant to be used daily. It has been laundered frequently and has that soft puckering which enhances the many rows of quilting worked on the surface by a very practised needlewoman. Though this was intended as a functional quilt, the maker carefully worked the whole surface with a clamshell quilting design.

Nine-patch c. 1880; **Feathered Star** c. 1890, Lockport, New York, Mrs. Robert McBride; **Pinwheel** c. 1900, Essex County, Ontario; **Hole-in-the-Barn-Door,** c. 1900, Barrie, Ontario, Minnie Hickling; **Pinwheel** c. 1920, origin unknown

SUMMER QUILTS OR COVERLETS

A few of these summer quilts, as they are called, have been included despite the fact they are not really quilts because they consist of only two layers of fabric, and sometimes only one.

The climate in Canada consists of four distinct seasons. In some areas the summer can be hot and humid, and lighter bedding is required. Hence, these pieced tops became known as summer quilts. The same amount of thought and care was expended on the piecing of a summer quilt as on a winter one. The pioneer woman took great pride in her quilts, as they gave colour to the decor of any room they graced. In the late 1800s, fabric became more available and life was a little easier. A well-appointed home had summer and winter curtains in addition to summer and winter quilts. Doorways were often draped with quilts and linen in the wintertime to keep out unwanted drafts. These would be removed in late spring to let the air circulate freely during the hot, humid summer months.

In England the fashion of unquilted coverlets endured until about 1830. Many pioneers had enjoyed these coverlets in their old homeland; it was only natural that they would utilize this technique in their new homeland. Immigrants soon discovered that winters were long and cold, houses were drafty, and fireplaces emitted not just heat but also unwanted black smoke that soiled curtains and bedding during the heating seasons. As laundry was a very time-consuming chore, only that which was essential was done during the winter months. Hence, winter quilts and curtains were usually dark in colour to conceal soot and soil.

Scrap Medallion c. 1827
Brockville, Ontario
Marion McCutcheon

*Details of **Scrap Medallion** showing manufacturers' stamp marks*

Marion McCutcheon came to Canada from Scotland in 1823 and settled in eastern Ontario. It is quite likely that she brought some fabrics with her when she immigrated, as you can see the Royal seal on one of the small pieces.

Medallion quilts were popular early in the nineteenth century, and often the centre square was more elaborately pieced than this one. Note that the surrounding borders were randomly pieced, utilizing even the minutest scraps of fabric. Fabric was expensive and scarce, so nothing was wasted. Upon careful examination, you can see that many of the border blocks have been seamed. The outer edges, including the selvages of the fabrics, have been used; the manufacturers' ink marks still show on some of the units.

This summer coverlet was never backed or quilted. It was probably used as a spread and was replaced when Marion was able to make another quilt using a larger inventory of scraps and possibly some new fabrics.

This is a wonderful example of block and roller prints that were available early in the 1800s. By the mid-nineteenth century, weaving was common in pioneer homes, and it was fashionable to have woven coverlets on many beds during the summer. Quilts were saved for the fall and winter months. Thus we do not see many summer quilts made during the late 1800s. Fortunately, some of the earlier ones, such as the one pictured, were stored in trunks away from light for many years, so they have survived in remarkably good condition. However, only fabric coverlets have been included in the discussion here, as weaving is another area of expertise.

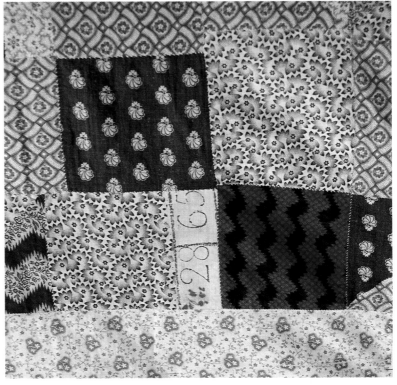

Cigar Ribbons *c. 1910*
Cowansville, Québec
Catherine Curley

Quilters have always had a consuming desire to save. Catherine Curley and her husband owned a hotel in Cowansville, Québec, and while cleaning the patrons' tables she became fascinated by the beauty of the ribbons that wrapped men's cigars. Over the years she collected these ribbons and decided to feather-stitch them into a tablecloth. The ribbons were of varying lengths, so Catherine was able to create a chevron design which did not require much trimming of the attractive ribbons.

Stripping was not a commonly used technique in the early 1900s, as quilters usually made Log Cabin blocks which required shorter strips of fabric than those used here. Catherine chose to feather-stitch the cigar ribbons onto a foundation, allowing her to control the angle of the units. Catherine was certainly innovative when it came to designing this top. She created the chevron units, which allowed her to use many shorter ribbons. Certainly, it must have taken a long period of time to collect sufficient ribbons of

varying lengths to create this exquisite tablecovering.

Unfortunately, many of the ribbons are starting to rot, but this interesting cloth has been a treasured table adornment for several generations of the Curley family.

MENNONITE TRADITIONS

Stars, Oxford County, Ontario

Some of the earliest settlers in Ontario were Mennonites. Many started to arrive from Pennsylvania after the American War of Independence. The first settlement in Ontario, in 1786, was located at The Twenty (later known as Jordan), a place where four families purchased 2,000 acres of land. The land had been previously given to Loyalists who fought for the British during the American Revolution. They had no interest in farming, so were selling their tracts of land for $2.50 an acre along the lake and $1.50 an acre inland. However, the land was not all in one block. Consequently, as time passed, the Mennonites in the Niagara Peninsula found it increasingly difficult to maintain their distinct society.

The Twenty became a stopping place for succeeding groups of immigrants coming north from Pennsylvania and other areas in the United States. Upon arriving at The Twenty, they were given food, shelter and an opportunity to rest before continuing on to other areas in the Niagara Peninsula or to areas farther west where it was possible to purchase fertile farmland for homesteading.

Newark (now Niagara-on-the-Lake) was the first capital of Upper Canada and the first Parliament sat at Navy Hall in 1792. The journey from Lancaster County, Pennsylvania, to Newark was about 400 miles through the Allegheny Mountains, across the Susquehanna River, through dense swamps, and then across the mighty Niagara River—an arduous journey for all those who attempted it. Some of those who led the way had compasses, but they also checked their routes by watching the stars at night. The Mennonites were God-fearing people; they watched the stars carefully and considered them "the eyes of God."

Here, on the gates of Navy Hall at Niagara-on-the-Lake, we see a well-worn antique Star quilt which has been handpieced. The quilting is very sparse, consisting of an overall "Ocean Wave" pattern. Resting on it are two rifles which were used by the Loyalist militia in the War of 1812.

1,000 Pyramids *c. 1920, Baden, Ontario, Laura Bricker*

Many of the first Mennonite settlers in Ontario were farmers. They arrived with the necessary tools and knowledge to plant seed crops and to construct barns and homes. The quilts in this section are from the collections of descendants of some of the earliest Mennonite settlers in Ontario. These descendants were very generous in sharing their personal records, thereby making it possible for me to compile the information contained in this section.

The Brickers were farmers for many generations in their communities in Lancaster County, Pennsylvania. The Coffmans are also descended from a long line of Pennsylvania farmers and preachers.

Samuel and John Bricker and family arrived in Ontario late in the spring of 1802. Available land was becoming scarce in the eastern United States, and like many other families, the Brickers had also suffered hardships inflicted on them by the Revolutionist sympathizers during the War of Independence. So, as news began to filter south from Canada that good farmland was available and

British Loyalists were welcome, many disillusioned and adventurous Mennonites started to move north. They hoped to start a new life and to enjoy religious and cultural freedom.

The Brickers heard that there was cheap land available in Waterloo County and decided to start their new life in a new country. It was a long and difficult journey, and upon arrival at The Twenty (now Jordan, Ontario), John's wife, Annie, took sick. She had to stay back while the two men went on to Waterloo County. Two weeks later they returned, each with a deed for 300 acres of land, which they had purchased from a Mr. Beasley for $1 per acre. The Brickers survived their first long, hard winter, and in the spring Sam travelled to York to purchase a new cow for his brother, John. There he was befriended by General Brock. The General helped Sam search the title to their land. Much to Sam's horror, he discovered that they did not have a clear title to their acreage. Upon the discovery that there was a £10,000 mortgage against the Beasley tract, the Bricker brothers

decided to enlist the help of their fellow brethren back in Pennsylvania.

Though Mennonites do not believe in communal ownership, they practise mutual aid, separation from the world, and church discipline. Sam felt it was the duty of those who could to help the settlers during this very difficult time. It took considerable persuasion, but he was eventually successful in securing the Mennonite brethren's help. The German Land Company was formed on November 28, 1803, by 23 farmers from Pennsylvania. They agreed to give Sam £10,000 to retire the mortgage on the 20,000 acres held by Mr. Beasley in Waterloo County. The money was entrusted to Sam in silver dollars and was put in a strong box that was placed under the seat of Sam's buggy, which he drove 500 miles through forests and swamps to Canada. Quite a responsibility for a young man! This arrangement guaranteed that a large tract of land would be subdivided and sold to future Mennonite arrivals from Pennsylvania.

The Coffmans saw their first glimpse of Waterloo County in 1882, when John Coffman came to assist the early settlers with their spiritual lives. He was an evangelical Mennonite preacher who was very successful at convincing young people to remain within the faith. Following in his footsteps, his son Fred also became an evangelical preacher. Fred settled in Vineland in 1902 after his marriage to Ella Mann.

The quilts on these pages represent many aspects of the Mennonite culture and spirituality. Quilts have always been important items in Mennonite homes. They were absolutely necessary as bedcoverings, and they afforded the only touch of colour inside the small, crowded log cabins. Colour and beauty have always been appreciated by

these plain people. They have colourful, well-tended gardens outside, and colourful, well-made quilts inside. None of their early quilts have survived; with regular use they eventually wore out. However, we are fortunate to have a representation here, and throughout the book, of quilts made by ancestors of one of the earliest visible minorities in Ontario.

The Charm quilt was made by Laura Bricker during the 1920s, when Charm quilts were very popular. To be a true Charm quilt, every piece used must be different, and most should be prints. Laura was well trained in needle skills by her mother. Throughout her life she made countless beautiful quilts that have been appreciated by Carol and her sister Helene Purdy.

The Nine-patch was made by Ida Pearl Bricker, Carol's mother. She created this colourful quilt using fabrics left over from the making of family clothing. Since the fabric scraps were somewhat drab, Ida chose a daisy print for the borders, sashings and the backing. This quilt, with its simple diagonal-X quilting in each block and pumpkin seed in the borders, was enjoyed by Carol during her growing years and then by her daughter. It shows signs of wear and age, so Carol has now taken it out of daily use and keeps it as a memento of the work lovingly done by her mother.

Nine-patch
Baden, Ontario
Ida Pearl Bricker

Here we see Carol McLean, one of Ontario's talented quilters and teachers. Carol is a direct descendant of John Bricker and is proud of her Mennonite heritage. Carol always has a small bag of quilt patches to work on while waiting for airplanes, children or professionals. In the photograph, she is piecing a Variable Star block, which seems to be a family favourite.

Carol has many happy memories of times spent with her Aunt Laura, who devoted numerous hours to helping Carol understand and execute the intricacies of piecing perfectly many small shapes into whole blocks. Both Laura and her mother, Isabelle, had enviable sewing skills which they learned at a very early age. Isabelle was a seamstress of some renown by the time she was 16. Since Laura's calling was to tend to her ailing mother during her lifetime, she never married, and thus Carol became the child she never had. A wonderful teacher, Laura believed the back of your work should look as fine as the front; if it is not correct, rip it out and redo it until it is perfect. Pride in her work showed in everything she did.

Carol is fortunate to have acquired some of her aunt's exquisite embroidery work, which adorns and protects a tabletop. She also has one of her aunt's large pincushions, which can be hung decoratively on the wall or propped functionally on a table near a favourite sewing chair, ever ready for quick daily repairs.

Carol enjoys perpetuating family quilting traditions while simultaneously experimenting to create new and innovative designs. She is lucky to have the two beautiful quilts on this page to remind her of the many happy hours spent learning and visiting with her aunt during her formative years. Indeed, Carol has since pursued

Carol McLean piecing a **Variable Star block**

Variable Star Quilt c. 1930
Baden, Ontario
Laura Bricker

her thirst for knowledge and has studied with many renowned quilting instructors and friends in North America, as well as teaching in Australia. When quilting experienced a rebirth in the mid-1970s, Carol came to the foreground both nationally and internationally as one of Canada's mosted practised and knowledgeable quilters.

The underlying design approach employed by most Mennonites, be they Old Order or Progressive, is simplicity—simplicity in colour, piecing and composition. Mennonites generally use few pure hues; muted hues are preferred. Their clothing is simple in style and colour, so their scrap fabrics provide a workable palette for the serious quilter. The small percentage of Old Order Mennonites and Amish who have chosen to pursue a simple, God-fearing life, devoid of the technological amenities of the twentieth century, still have large scrap inventories of dark, heavy

fabrics which are used in outer clothing. These scraps naturally find their way into some of their quilts, as they still require warm bedcovering during the winter months. However, even some of these winter quilts were colourful, as can be seen in the Pineapple Log Cabin quilt found on page 122.

Clothing scraps, when carefully selected, can make an effective two-colour quilt. Laura Bricker, Carol's aunt, used an assortment of navy and white or black and white clothing scraps for this precisely pieced quilt. In each design block, all the identical shapes are the same print, which gives some continuity to each Star Sampler block. The light sashing binds the design, which is bordered and quilted with assorted straight-line quilting motifs.

Laura used blue tailor's chalk to mark her quilting design on the sashing and border. Having never washed out, it is still quite visible and now gives the quilt another dimension of charm and character.

To make this design, Laura would first have sorted her fabrics into lights, mediums and darks. Each block has the same colour intensity as the one in the matching location. Since the colours around the edge of each design element are darks and mediums, Laura had no choice but to sash her blocks with a light print. Notice that great care was taken to be certain that any stripes or one-way design fabrics always went in the same direction.

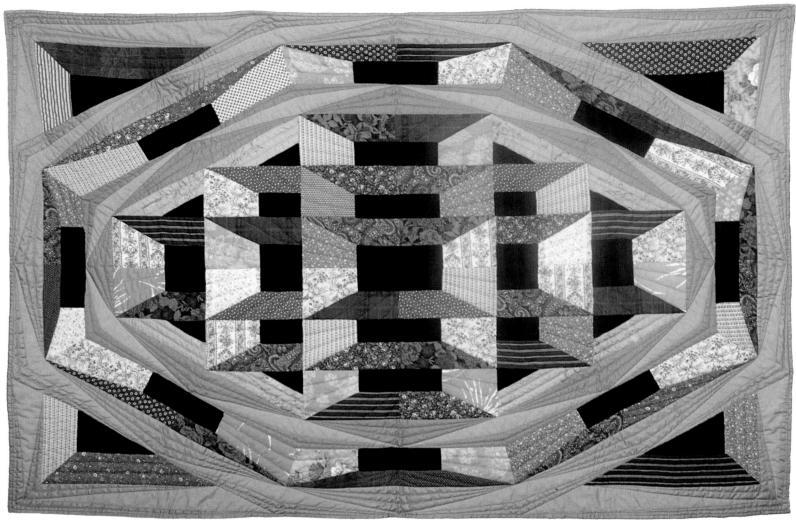

Viewpoint Galactica 1988
Woodstock, Ontario
Carol McLean

Here we see Viewpoint Galactica, Carol's wall quilt, perfectly pieced, utilizing some soft-coloured scraps. It has been completed using simple quilting lines to enhance her complex piecing design.

Carol builds on a solid tradition of simplicity of colour and design, but employs contemporary design concepts and tools. She creates quilts that are innovative while satisfying a basic desire for something beautiful. Canada is fortunate to have in Carol both a teacher and a quilt artist!

Detail of **Viewpoint Galactica**

Pride in their workmanship is evident in all the projects undertaken within the Mennonite community. Ellen was a young woman when her mother had Mrs. Lavina Honsberger of Vineland, Ontario, make this peacock Whole Cloth quilt for her. Lavina was very active in her church, so the quilting, which was done using a deep pink thread, was probably executed by the ladies of the Women's Missionary Society.

While simplicity is the rule for Mennonite clothing, it does *not* rule out the use of colour—discretion is the key. Ellen was fond of green, so her mother had this sateen Whole Cloth quilt made for her in her favourite colours. It was undoubtedly part of her trousseau. However, Ellen did not marry. She was educated as a nurse and worked at this career all her working life. This beautiful quilt certainly would have been used by Ellen as a spread on her bed to be viewed and enjoyed, then turned down or removed when it was time to retire.

Crazy quilts have long been a favourite of skilled needlewomen. The craze began in the Victorian era, and we see here that the technique is an effective way of displaying an assortment of cherished scraps enhanced by stitching and embroidery skills.

Like his father and grandfather before him, Samuel Fred Coffman was a Mennonite evangelist dedicated to helping people live a vital spiritual life and to giving a more effective Christian witness in this world. Conducting marriages was an important and emotional experience. It was often a time of baptism into the faith as well as a union of two committed people. Fred, as he was generally called, collected snippets of fabric from the brides' wedding dresses and added to these a piece of his own wedding suit, his wife's wedding dress and his mother's wedding

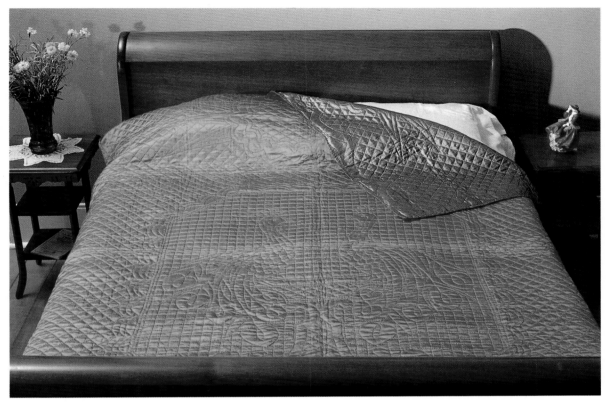

Whole Cloth Peacock Motif *c. 1930, Vineland, Ontario, Mrs. Lavina Honsberger*

dress. There was a legend which was kept with this quilt for many years, but unfortunately it has been lost. His daughters recall that the first four numbers denote the following: 1) Magdalena was Fred's mother; 2) the black fabric is from Fred's wedding suit; 2) the grey-blue fabric is from Ella Mann's wedding dress; 3) pieces were used from Mrs. Page's wedding dress (Mrs. Page and her husband were among the first Mennonite missionaries to go to India); and 4) Melinda (Mann) King, aunt to the Coffman girls, now owns and treasures this quilt.

Mrs. C.P. Watson of Vineland took the special pieces of fabric which Fred had collected and pieced them together using the traditional feather-stitch and an assortment of coloured embroidery floss. Each patch was carefully

numbered and one was dated 1911. She then bordered it with a Flying Geese motif from her scrap bag. As on many special quilts, a flounce was added using the same fabric as the backing. Like most Crazy quilts, this one has no batting. It was meant to be used as a spread rather than a functional quilt; as a coverlet, it has no quilting.

This coverlet has long been cherished by the family and is now brought out only on special occasions. It is a wonderful example of the type of fabrics used in Mennonite clothing during the early 1900s.

Crazy *1911*
Vineland, Ontario
Mrs. P.C. Watson

The Pineapple Log Cabin is one of the most difficult Log Cabin sets, so this variation was usually used only for very special quilts. Sharing and giving is part of the Mennonite culture. Like his father and grandfather before him, Fred travelled extensively in both the United States and Canada, helping people to organize churches in their areas. It was during his travels, prior to his 1901 marriage to Ella, that he was presented with this very colourful Log Cabin quilt.

This quilt has been well used and much enjoyed. Unfortunately, the brown fabric was not of the same quality as the others. It is the only fabric that succumbed to wear, mainly along the edges, where it was probably tucked under the feather tick. The fabric for the lining was dyed by the ladies of the parish. Being very resourceful people, they were familiar with dyeing, and recipes for various dye colours would have been shared among members of a congregation.

This quilt has been very simply quilted once around the design, halfway out from the centre and once around each block.

Often Mennonite designs are simple in their use of colour and fabrics. It is interesting to compare this Mennonite version of Pineapple Log Cabin with the one on page 79, where the quilter had a large palette of fabrics from which to work.

Some patterns are also favoured by church groups who quilt together. They spend considerable time perfecting their templates and then enjoy making many different combinations of a certain design.

Within the Mennonite community there were always a few women who would piece or mark quilts for clients and then the Women's Missionary Society could be commissioned to do the quilting.

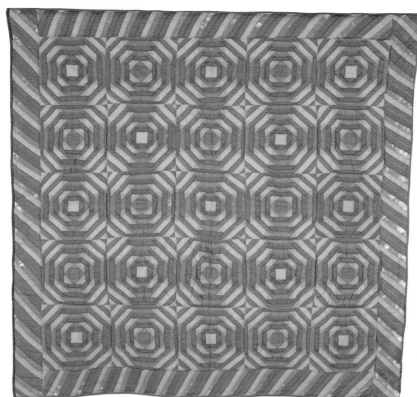

Pineapple Log Cabin c. 1901
Virginia

Paper-cut Appliqué
Vineland, Ontario
Women's Missionary Society of Moyer Mennonite Church

Here we have two wonderful examples of a variation on a theme. Both of these quilts have been carefully machine-appliquéd with perfectly blending thread. It was no easy feat to move the fabric through a treadle sewing machine and keep the stitches uniform. Isabelle McLaughlin certainly had mastered the idiosyncrasies of her sewing machine, as her appliqué stitching is almost flawless.

The red-and-white quilt has had a border added for extra interest, and Isabelle even gave the corners special treatment. The Women's Missionary Society of the Moyer Mennonite Church then quilted this top with intersecting circles. The red fabric is a deep black-red. One has to wonder whether it was commercially dyed using "cochineal" red pigment or one of the new synthetic dyes. (Cochineal was made from the dried bodies of a female insect that lives on cactus plants.)

General Store in Vineland, Ontario, c. 1930

The blue-and-white quilt is simpler in design but has a variety of quilting motifs. The tulips have been outline-quilted as well as embellished within the motifs. The ladies of the Moyer Mennonite Church Women's Missionary Society were very accomplished quilters, as evidenced by their uniform stitches throughout both quilts.

Vineland was a bustling community and here we see the general store where community members shopped. Motor cars were becoming more popular and this postcard provides a glimpse of life as it was at The Twenty circa 1930.

Crazy quilts were very special quilts in any household in which they were found. Laura Bricker made this one around 1920.

Laura was a young woman already betrothed when her mother fell ill with diabetes and became a semi-invalid for the remainder of her life. As was customary at that time, Laura was required to break her engagement and devote her life to caring for her ill mother and tending to the household. Niece Carol can remember visiting her Aunt Laura as a young girl and having her aunt open her hope chest and share with her the beautiful linens she had made for her future home, which, of course, she never had.

Laura was well trained in needle skills by her mother, and as her life evolved she had more and more time to devote to her favourite pastime.

Crazy quilts are always Scrap quilts which have been lovingly created and evoke a wealth of memories. Often they were kept for special guests or used as a "good" quilt on the maker's bed when company was visiting. Whatever the intended purpose of this quilt, Laura carefully embroidered her patches with variegated embroidery yarn, using the favoured feather stitch. She finished her top with a cotton sateen ruffle. This is a lightweight quilt with *no* batting, rather the three layers of fabric have been carefully quilted with dark thread, using a square motif. The quilting has been deliberately kept sparse so as not to detract from the piecing.

It is quite likely that Laura would have "dressed up" her bed with this very special quilt that is now enjoyed by her niece.

Not only does Carol design and make quilts, she also collects them. In 1981, while attending an auction in Woodstock, she purchased this Sampler for $37.50.

Crazy Quilt c. 1920, Baden, Ontario, Laura Bricker

Detail showing homespun backing and ruffle on **Crazy Quilt**

One can only speculate about the maker, but the fabrics have not been organized into shades and little care was taken with the placement of the blocks. It can be assumed that this quilt was made by an inexperienced quilter, perhaps as a learning quilt for a young sewer. It has been handpieced except for the binding, which is the back brought to the front, turned in and machine-stitched.

This appealing Sampler has been quilted by several people, probably at a quilting bee, as the quilting stitches are of varying sizes and uniformity. It has been used very little and is in excellent condition. Perhaps its creator saved it for its sentimental value as one of her first quilts.

Sampler, origin unknown

Here we see a pair of quilts made by Isabelle Bricker. These two predominantly woollen quilts were made for cold weather. On the bed is a Star Medallion which has been precisely pieced. Careful use has been made of the blue fabric which has been sparingly scattered throughout the top. It gives just a little sparkle to what is intended to be a warm, functional quilt. This quilt has a very thin cotton batting and a thin plaid lining. Isabelle certainly enjoyed working with fabrics and colours. She also made an attempt to shade the yarns which she used to tie this quilt. Perhaps she was using up scrap yarns as well as scrap fabrics, but, if so, she certainly was careful of their colour placement.

On the chair is a Folded Log Cabin quilt known as Streak O' Lightning. Every log in this quilt has a small fold in it, which was done to give added warmth. Bedrooms became particularly cool at night as fires died down, so it was necessary to have a warm quilt on every bed in the household. It is interesting to observe that blue seemed to be a special colour in both quilts. It has been used differently as an accent colour in each. Isabelle's blue-and-

black border on her Star quilt serves to frame and highlight the central design. The quilt has no batting and several squares in each block have been quilted "in the ditch" in order to hold the three layers of fabric together.

While the age of these quilts is not known, it is assumed by family members that the Log Cabin quilt is older than the Star Medallion and both would have been made by the turn of the century.

Isabelle Doering Bricker lived in Baden, Ontario, where her family settled after immigrating to Canada from Cumberland County, Pennsylvania. The Brickers were originally Pennsylvania Mennonites whose clothes would have been made from the assortment of navy-and-white prints found in this perfectly pieced quilt. Some time after the family immigrated, they broke away from the Old Order Mennonite lifestyle. It is not known whether this occurred because they married outside of the faith or because they desired a more progressive lifestyle.

The subtle neutral colours of this quilt are pleasingly accented with red. The red sprigged muslin has been used in all the blocks, but

Double-X c. 1900, Baden, Ontario, Laura Bricker

the background fabrics change. The blocks with the darker background have been used in the corner areas. The border squares have been carefully cut and seamed from a black and white stripe pattern which runs in one direction on the sides and another direction along the top and

Streak O' Lightning
Baden, Ontario
Isabelle Doering Bricker
Star Medallion ("slashed squares"/triangle borders) c. 1900
Baden, Ontario
Isabelle Doering Bricker

bottom, providing added interest. The dark-red border frames the central area, and the simple clean-cut appearance of this Double-X design has been maintained by "in the ditch" quilting through the middle of the sashing and a diagonal line through the plain blocks.

Beauty and colour are characteristics common to all quilts exhibited in this section. Today Mennonites are still very proud of their quilts and continue to enjoy these beautiful bedcoverings in their homes.

THE QUILTING BEE

The quilting bee was an important activity for the pioneer woman. It afforded her an opportunity to visit with her peers, share ideas about quilt designs, and trade quilt patterns, while getting tips for household chores and advice on caring for the sick. All this while simultaneously quilting a top.

Not only were quilting bees social occasions, they were also supportive endeavours both emotionally and physically. For those living in remote rural areas, they alleviated some of the isolation as well as providing relief from the drudgery of daily life. Generally, an invitation was required if the bee was for a special quilt. For a wedding or presentation quilt, the area's best quilters were invited.

Whenever tragedy such as a fire struck, the ladies of the community would come together and make quilts and other necessities to ease the suffering of their friends.

The Quilting Party, *by Harold W. McCrea, Canadian 1887-1969, Art Gallery of Ontario, gift of the estate of Lady Eaton, 1977*

Floral Appliqué 1991
St. Catharines, Ontario
The Winchester Cross Quilters of
St. George's Anglican Church

Historically, quilting bees have been a time of camaraderie, a time to share of ideas and snippets of gossip while simultaneously working on the current quilt. Many churches throughout Ontario have quilting groups. This group was celebrating its 106th birthday the day they were photographed working on their most recent quilt, a floral appliqué that will eventually be raffled to raise funds for the church. In the background is a commissioned Pieced quilt which had just been completed.

The ladies quilt every Tuesday from 10 a.m. until 2:30 p.m., stopping only briefly for lunch. As they are accomplished quilters, their stitches are all uniform. It is impossible to find any discrepencies in stitch lengths even though the quilt is worked on by various women

In small communities the church has long been the focus of the social life of its members. Even in large metropolitan areas, church quilting groups still provide opportunities for socializing. The Winchester Cross Quilters group of St. George's Anglican Church in St. Catharines, Ontario, is no exception.

EMBROIDERED QUILTS

Pink blossoms, babies, young girls, love—all conjure up thoughts of spring. This cross-stitch quilt was lovingly made by a grandmother in western Ontario and given to her newborn granddaughter many years ago. The granddaughter has enjoyed it all her life, and now she too is learning the art of quilting.

The pattern was placed onto the blocks by hot iron transfers and the design was worked in pink cross-stitch and satin stitch. The quilt was bordered with pink to give it a feminine appearance. It has been photographed here with an antique doll sitting in a carriage on a beautiful spring day.

After a long day's work many farm women enjoyed sitting and embroidering in the evening. Jane Lang Elmhirst of Otonabee Township in eastern Ontario embroidered 15 floral blocks as well as partial blocks for the border of this quilt. The blocks have been defined with red sashing and set on the point for added interest. Superimposed over the design is a symmetrical leaf quilting motif which extends from corner to corner.

By the twentieth century, home decorating was more colourful and quilts that were not used on a daily basis adorned many dining-room tables.

Floral Embroidery c. 1910
Otonabee Township, Ontario
Jane Lang (Elmhirst) McIntyre

Embroidered Flower Baskets 1965
Wilberforce, Ontario
Margaret (Maggie) McMahon

Summers are generally warm in southern Ontario, so quilts with batting are not required. Embroidery was a popular means of creating a summer spread with sufficient body to drape properly on a bed. It afforded a change in room decor when housecleaning was completed, winter quilts removed and summer linens put into circulation.

It is interesting to study the designs used. They have appeared in many quilts and coverlets in Ontario, and almost without fail, the embroidery is done with red thread. Some of the designs for these quilts were bought as transfers, while others were copied from some of the popular embroidery magazines that were then available. This embroiderer was proud of her skills and dated two blocks used here.

This piece also has many animal blocks which seem to have been very popular during the era, and the good-luck horseshoe has been added at every intersection. To give the spread a finished appearance, this talented needle-woman embroidered a variety of designs around the perimeter of her summer quilt, which has been sparsely quilted to a backing fabric of muslin.

Embroidered Sampler 1905, *origin unknown*

Cortecilli *magazine displaying some advertisements for threads*

The family history on this quilt is incomplete, but the last McKee who owned it tells us that it was made by an 10-year-old girl, using woollen yarn that was dyed from plants found on the land where the family lived. It was owned by several generations of McKees before being purchased by its present owner. While it was made by a young girl, it has always been treated as an heirloom. Only occasionally would it be taken out of its chest to be viewed by the children. It is known that the McKees emigrated from Ireland in 1837 and settled in Smith Township in Peterborough County. As the quilt is dated 1840, there is no doubt that it was made here in Ontario.

The yarn used for the embroidery is very fine and could have been doubled and twisted had the embroiderer been more experienced and/or had more yarn. The central area has been carefully worked with birds and flowers and is surrounded by the following phrases:

Home, home sweet sweet home
Dear Saviour in glory my home
ten thousand to
their endless home.
This solemn moment fly and come
and soon expect to die

Studying this quilt, one has to wonder if Bevin knew that she had a terminal illness. She probably spent much of her time working alone on this quilt, as other family members would have had chores to complete. Working on this quilt helped Bevin to pass the many long and lonely hours of physical suffering and turmoil of mind which she probably endured during her short life. It also explains why this quilt was so treasured by the succeeding generations of McKees who owned it.

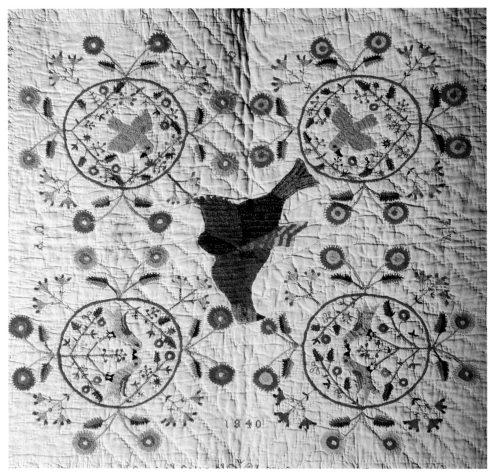

*Detail of **Embroidered Scripture Quilt** 1840 shown on page 129*
Peterborough County, Ontario
Bevin McKee

To the left of the central medallion is the date 1840 and at the right side opposite the date is the number ten. We also see the symbols for alpha and omega at the bottom centre, which symbolize the beginning and the end—this young child was exhibiting her thoughts in this embroidery. One wonders where she got her inspirations for the designs. Were they in an embroidery book brought from the Old Country and then altered by Bevin as her imagination allowed? She used many bird motifs and the central bird seems to be wearing a scarf.

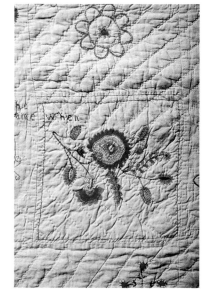

*Detail of **Embroidered Scripture Quilt** showing embroidery motif*

Detail showing Hi A Wa Tha

Embroidered Sampler *1895*
Burgessville, Ontario
Alberta Buchanan

Detail showing Horse's Head

Alberta Buchanan enjoyed embroidery and probably got these patterns through a mail-order source from one of the many farm weekly magazines. Like many other quilters, she assembled her collection of embroidered blocks into a quilt. Alberta wanted her embroidery to be sufficiently dense to show on the surface of the block, so she used a thick floss and worked her design with the stem stitch.

We know that these designs were transferred onto the fabric with a hot iron, as some of the dots are still visible. Alberta then proceeded with the embroidery. These transfer designs were popular for about 15 years. This one is dated 1895. Other quilts in this section have later dates.

When the block featuring the native chief was transferred onto the fabric, the image was reversed. This was immaterial to the figure, but the letters were reversed. The detail picture shows the block as it was intended to be embroidered and the inscription reads "Hi A Wa Tha." Hiawatha was a legendary chief of the Onondaga tribe.

Here we see a beautiful dated reversible quilt. Mrs. Bain probably got her embroidery patterns from the farm weekly. We see these designs on quilts appearing on this page and also on page 131. Such designs were readily available and quite popular during the 1890s and early 1900s. The quilts were almost always executed with red embroidery floss on a white background. However, in this special quilt, we see that Mrs. Bain embroidered one side, while the other side is a pieced Sawtooth design dated May 23, 1892. All the piecing for this quilt was executed by hand. Considering that the triangles are only slightly more than 1 inch per side and that there are a multitude of them in this design, Mary must have spent hundreds of hours cutting and piecing. The quilting is a simple square grid superimposed over the whole surface.

Traditionally, quilts were made only as bedding. It was unusual to be so well supplied as to have the luxury of this exquisite reversible quilt.

Two-sided quilt: **Embroidered Sampler, Sawtooth** *1892*
Petrolia, Ontario
Mrs. Bain

Sawtooth - *back of two-sided quilt*
(front shown above)

ly machine-embroidered motif in the central area. This was worked on the top with a variety of machine-embroidery stitches before it was backed and batted. The design was outlined during the quilting process, so it appears as a simple drawing on the back side. The design was first drawn onto the fabric with a pencil, and in some areas where the quilter wandered slightly, the pencil marks are still visible. This is a wonderful study of continuous-line quilting, as it appears that only in the two box motif rings did the quilter have to stop and start, and she did two of these in each step.

Over the years, quilts were reversed in order to preserve the "design side." Usually the backs of quilts were not very interesting, since they were made to be used and replaced when worn out. However, this quilt was a gift of love, and much care was put into its design and execution. The reverse side makes a very beautiful Whole Cloth quilt, which means that this quilt can be enjoyed no matter which side is facing up.

*Whole Cloth c. 1950 Korea; **Pine Burr** c. 1920 (bed) eastern Ontario; **Hexagon** (Grandmother's Flower Garden) c. 1930, Amherstburg, Ontario, Mrs. Maurice Foy*

On the bed you can see a quilt from eastern Ontario made from fabric that was home-dyed using onion skins and marigolds. This colour was popular in rural areas, as it was one that was easy to create and was very stable. The pattern is known as Pine Burr, and it was completely handpieced and quilted in 1920 using a diagonal grid.

It is possible that this attractive quilt was made as a gift, since it is perfectly pieced and the recipient took such good care of it that it is in mint condition even though it is 70-plus years old.

On the table is a 1930 Hexagon variation referred to as Grandmother's Flower Garden. True to tradition, this is an all-cotton Scrap quilt that was made to be used. Now that the fabrics are deteriorating, it is displayed on a table, where it will get minimal wear.

Machine-quilting has been practised by a few people since the sewing machine was invented. Here is a perfectly executed 1950 Whole Cloth quilt that has been "freely" machine-quilted as a complete work of art. Hung above the bed is what was meant to be the back side of a quilt which was quilted with dark grey thread. Upon careful examination you can see where the top red thread has been pulled through, probably when the designer was changing bobbins. Little is known about this quilt except that it was presented to Dr. F. Murray, a United Church medical missionary in Korea during the years 1921-1969. It was probably made by one of the church parishioners, a very skilled needlewoman, on behalf of the congregation.

The front side of this exquisite quilt features red thread against orange fabric and has a complete-

*Front of machine embroidered **Whole Cloth** quilt c. 1950, Korea; shown on wall above*

During the 1930s, Tudor architecture was popular in some urban areas of Ontario. Building supplies were reasonably available, as were talented artisans. The two ornate quilts pictured here are reminiscent of a bygone era when embroidery and handpiecing were enjoyed by many family members. The mirror (c. 1900) was originally in the Royal York Hotel in Toronto. Here it reflects the ornately embroidered Mock Cathedral Window quilt displayed on the banister.

Eliza Ann Evans used sugar bags as her foundation and then carefully embroidered her collection of silk scraps onto the foundation blocks using gold embroidery floss and feather stitching. The blocks were seamed using the same thread and feather stitching. This elaborate quilt was undoubtedly saved for special guests or displayed over a sofa or banister, as it is shown here.

The Log Cabin quilt on the wall was also made by Eliza Ann Evans and is one of her early endeavours. Her parents owned a hotel in Mount Forest, a stage-coach stop on the route between Guelph and Owen Sound. Many of the logs for this quilt were cut from silk ties or other "dress" fabrics. It is possible that many of the guests gave her discarded ties or dress scraps when they passed through. The silks in this Barn Raising Log Cabin give the quilt a shimmer and a feeling of luxury which is further enhanced by the gilded mirror hanging on the wall of this spacious hallway.

Both of these quilts have been carefully tied to the back so as not to detract from the piecing of the top, a technique which was frequently used on Crazy quilts.

Magic Circles c. 1930 (also known as *Moon and Stars*), *Mount Forest, Ontario, Eliza Ann Evans;* **Log Cabin, Barn Raising** c. 1930, *Mount Forest, Ontario, Eliza Ann Evans*

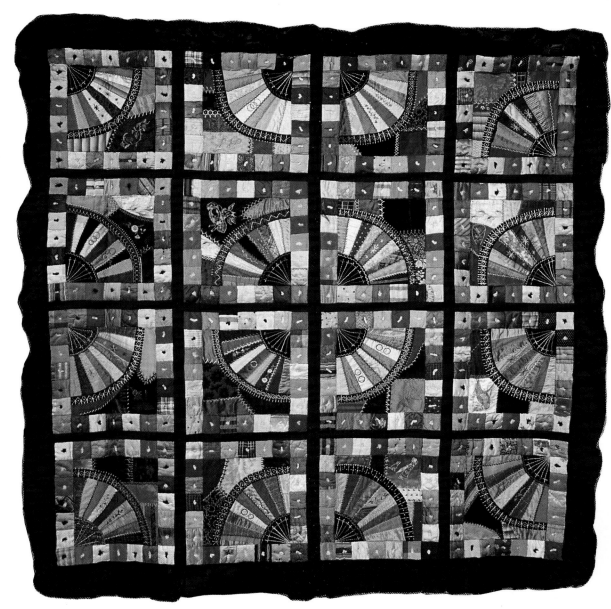

To the observer, the process whereby the quilter selects an arrangement for her scraps is often a mystery. This quilter liked stuffed work, so all the squares which surround the fans have been stuffed and tied to the foundation. The fan motif afforded the creator an opportunity to use a large number of scraps without having to worry about size—hardly any of the spokes of the fan are the same size. Embroidery was used extensively by this quilter;

the blocks are heavily embroidered with a variety of designs. The central area was carefully worked. There is a realistic owl watching the world, as well as the maker's initials, L.E.P. This piece has been carefully quilted "in the ditch" (in the seam line) in the rows of sashing.

Since the quilt is so ornately worked and initialled, it is likely that it was meant to be proudly displayed on the guest bed.

While this is a Scrap quilt, it

gives the same visual impression as a Crazy quilt where the irregular patches are embroidered together. The design took considerable planning, with careful organization of scraps as to size and colour. Since the quilt is made almost exclusively from silks, I suspect that the maker or a relative was working in the garment industry; she apparently had a large inventory of luxurious scraps.

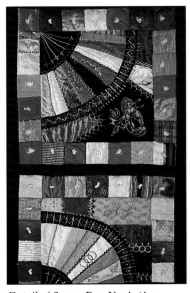

*Detail of **Scrap Fan Variation**
showing piecing and embroidery*

HEXAGON OR HONEYCOMB QUILTS

Octagon Mosaic c. 1930, Wheatley, Ontario, Cleda Holland

These Hexagon or Octagon quilts are simple to make, since the shapes are usually sewn over a paper pattern. This keeps the geometric angles and edges in line. The individual nature of the rosettes allows practically unlimited colour variations. Honeycomb quilts were popular in England from the late 1700s. In the January 1835 issue of *Godey's Lady's Book*, published in Philadelphia, instructions for a Honeycomb quilt read as follows:

1. Cut out a piece of pasteboard the size you intend to make the patches.
2. Lay this model on your calico and cut your patches of the same shape, allowing a little larger all around for turning in at the edges. Of course the patches must be all exactly the same size.
3. Get some stiff papers (old copy books or letters will do) and cut them also into hexagons precisely the size of the pasteboard model.
4. Prepare as many of these papers as you have patches.
5. Baste or tack a patch upon every paper, turning down the edge of the calico over the wrong side.
6. Sew together neatly over the edge, 6 of these patches, so as to form a ring. Then sew together 6 or more in the same manner, and so on until you have enough. Let each ring consist of the same sort of calico, or at least the same colour. The papers must be left in to keep the patches in shape till the whole is completed.

These were indeed complete and explicit instructions. *Godey's Lady's Book* was widely read and its patterns shared in both Canada and the United States. These instructions are still appropriate for anyone wishing to handpiece a Honeycomb quilt today.

A graphic Scrap Octagon variation has been created by piecing a small square of contrasting fabric across the corners of two diagonally opposite blocks. This colourful quilt was made in the early 1930s, when the Depression made life difficult and people were under considerable stress. Quilts were necessary for bedcovering, and the creative woman used her colours effectively to add brightness to her daily existence.

Cleda Holland used whatever scraps she had to create a pleasing colour arrangement. We see an assortment of cottons, flannelettes and a bright, colourful print border contained by the same bright red used in the small blocks in the central design.

The quilting is in a simple diagonal line, a technique which holds the layers of fabric and batting together. True to tradition, the backing is flannelette, so the quilt does not slip off the bed during the night.

Special quilts were left to special relatives. In her will, Cleda left this quilt to her niece so that there would be no question as to what would happen to it after her death.

Hex Star c. 1900
Yorkshire, England

This sensational Hexagon—a favourite of the English quilter—was pieced in Yorkshire, England, in the late 1800s. An assortment of available chintzes was utilized. Chintzes were expensive, but they afforded the quilter an unexpected dimension in scale, colour and texture. Not only did this quilter have a wonderful sense of colour, but she certainly knew how to organize her hexagons so as to outline the various angled sections of the overall design.

These Hexagon quilts are always handpieced, and it is quite likely that the quilter had the over-all Hex Star design in mind when she started this top. She would have pieced it in sections and then sewn the sections together. It is a very large quilt for its era (112 by 109 inches), so it may have been a group project. Upon completion of the top, each side was turned under almost 10 inches and hemmed, giving excellent "body" and a lovely finished appearance to the quilt when it adorns the appropriate bed. It is possible that this was a summer coverlet, as it is not backed, rather the edges have only been turned under and stitched.

This early 1900s Hexagon quilt is a tessellated design utilizing a 1-inch hexagon. Margaret Farr enjoyed handpiecing and the blue sprigged muslin has been featured in every unit throughout. The turkey red, which appears in the centres as well as in the sashing, was frugally used, as some of the centre units were carefully pieced.

Quilters did not always worry about matching thread to the colour of their fabric. White thread was always in supply. This quilt was completely pieced using white thread, which now shows through in the red areas. The fabric has shrunk with repeated washings, which has put some stress on the seams. Margaret chose to use a clamshell design for her quilting, which gives the overall surface texture and depth without detracting from its strong graphic appearance.

This graphic three-colour Mosaic quilt has been displayed over a late nineteenth-century pine armoire to enhance the room's decor.

Hexagon Diamonds c. 1920
Grey County, Ontario
Margaret Farr

138

Mosaics were always handpieced, as they were sewn over a paper template. You can observe the construction of this quilt from the detail, which shows that the owner left the templates in along the outer edge. These templates were made from letters, invoices and other papers that were no longer needed. Upon close examination we can see dates such as 1896, 1898, a Guelph 1889 postal cancellation stamp, and some very uniform penmanship.

Emmaline Roy was the maker of this Scrap Mosaic quilt. The town of Royston was named after the Roys, who had the first mill, powered by Royston Creek. They supplied the small settlement with building materials. Emmaline chose her fabrics carefully. This quilt was made as a wedding gift for her brother, James, and his bride, and was given to them in 1908. One can only wonder why it was never completed. Certainly, as the years passed, the templates in the back of this top made the back of the quilt as interesting as the front.

While the design is often referred to as Mosaic, it does remind one of a meadow of flowers, hence the name Grandmother's Flower Garden is often used for this arrangement of blocks.

Mosaic c. 1908
Royston, Ontario
Emmaline Roy

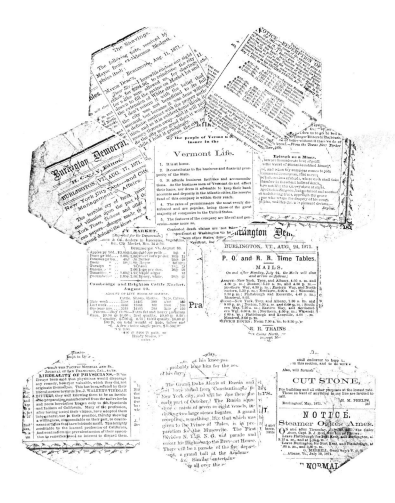

Details of templates used in
Grandmother's Flower Garden *c. 1872*
shown on page 7
Fletcher, Vermont
Mrs. Charles Webster

In the 1870s, log cabins were prevalent in both Vermont and Ontario. While this top was photographed in Ontario, it was actually pieced in Vermont and still has many of the template shapes in it. It was so dirty that the present owner felt it had to be cleaned, so many papers were removed. A few of the templates have been included here, since they tell us as much about Vermont life in the late 1800s as the quilt tells us about its maker.

The templates were used only as a mechanism to press over the seam allowance and add some stiffness to the fabric until the units were actually seamed. Piecing Mosaic quilts was tedious and time-consuming. Often a quilter would lose interest in the project before it was completed. Many of these tops ended up in trunks, only to be discovered many years later by family members.

It is known that this top was made by a Mrs. Charles Webster of Fletcher, in Franklin County, Vermont. However, when the records were checked, there was no trace of this woman. At the moment, it is speculated that she might have lived her later years with a married daughter whose surname would have been different. Records do show Websters living in other areas of Vermont, so one might assume that she moved to Fletcher to be with family after she was widowed.

Here we have an intricate Hexagon top made by William Darling, who served as a Welsh fusilier in India during the 1880s. Upon his discharge from service, William filled his days by piecing this spectacular top, whose hexagons are a scant 1 inch across. He probably made himself one metal template which he used to cut his shapes and another smaller one to crease the heavy felted wool to the finished size.

The number of uniforms used in making this top will never be known, but it is interesting to note that William tried to use as much of the red from a uniform as possible. Upon close examination one can see the staining and wear of the fabric. Army surplus stores have been in existence almost as long as there have been wars, and it is likely that William obtained what additional fabric he required for this top at one of these stores. His family tells us that he used his own uniform in this top and had to augment the fabric, probably with purchased fabric. However, all the fabric is of the same weight and quality.

The top was pieced in sections, which were then sewn together and backed. William chose a colourful print to back this top. It was imperative that the top be backed to prevent it from stretching hopelessly out of shape. The present owners have been especially careful with this top because the outer edges have been neither backed nor finished.

Mosaic c. 1880, origin unknown, William Darling

Details of quilt seen on page 141 showing colourful printed backing; perfect piecing is clearly visible.

When this spectacular top is reversed it is possible to view how William assembled it. He did not press his units over a paper template, rather he carefully marked his seam lines and pressed the units over a smaller metal template. These units have been carefully and precisely pieced together. Yellow thread has been used in the seaming of many of the units, but because of the density of the fabric it does not show on the right side.

The colourful printed back has been meticuously seamed and invisibly tacked to the top in the finished areas. It is only along the unfinished edge that you can observe how the two layers were basted together.

This coverlet has been so accurately pieced that even after all these years there is almost no distortion in it—amazing, considering its weight.

DOUBLE WEDDING RING & DRESDEN PLATE

Double Wedding Ring has been a favourite pattern of needlewomen young and old throughout this century. It has frequently been made as part of a trousseau or given as a wedding gift to some fortunate young couple.

Isabel Johnston, utilizing family dress scraps and assisted by her mother, made this quilt when she was a teenager. While the scraps are fairly bright, the intersecting diamonds have been pieced from a soft yellow and peach, which draws your eye to the diamond of the wedding ring. Isabel was not the accomplished quilter that she is now, so her mother advised her to outline-quilt the motif and quilt diamonds in the open areas. A more experienced quilter would have done elaborate quilting in the open areas. However, Isabel spent many happy hours working on this family heirloom and daydreaming about what life had in store for her.

Dresden Plate became a popular pattern during the 1930s and has continued to be a favoured pattern, especially for church groups making quilts to be raffled. Mrs. Wilson pieced this Scrap variation, which has a green accent used in the plates and for the border. The centre of each plate was constructed by appliquéing four elliptical shapes onto the foundation block. The border was constructed by alternately piecing green and white plate-shaped pieces together. The white shape is always inverted and when completed the border unit is straightened.

Mrs. Wilson was an active mem-ber of the quilting group at Paris United Church, so it is possible that the ladies had a quilting bee and did crosshatch quilting to complete this popular design. This cheerful quilt is still being displayed and enjoyed by family members.

Also on display here are three other Scrap quilts, all of the same era, exhibiting an array of fabrics and quilt designs frequently used by quilters.

On the right is an Ohio Star design made by Mrs. George Lockhart. When Mrs. Lockhart died, this Scrap quilt was destined for the garbage, from whence it was rescued by its present owners. Not all family members appreciate quilts for their warmth and light-ness as well as for their interesting array of colourful fabric scraps.

On the left we see the popular Double Wedding Ring, this one made by Martha Cunningham. It is presently owned and treasured by her granddaughter, a quilt enthusiast and teacher in eastern Ontario.

The third quilt is featured and described on page 24.

Dresden Plate c. 1940
Paris, Ontario
Double Wedding Ring c. 1940
Walton, Ontario
Martha Cunningham
Ohio Star
Ingersoll, Ontario
Mrs. George Lockhart

Double Wedding Ring 1938
Ottawa, Ontario
Isabel Johnston

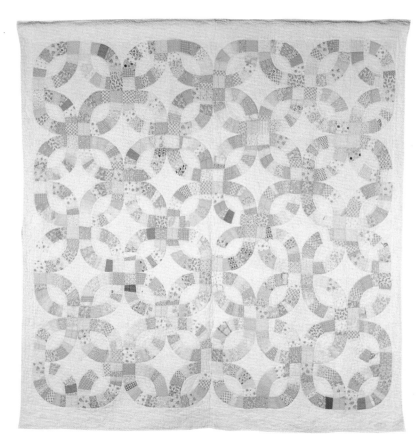

Double Wedding Ring c. 1940
Vineland, Ontario

These quilts are wonderful examples of the fabrics that were available in the area. Often many of the scraps used had special memories for the quilt's recipient. This quilt has been well used and has some worn areas, so it has been taken out of circulation and saved for succeeding generations to enjoy.

Mary Elizabeth Hyland made this quilt in 1935 at the age of 74. It was a wedding gift for her special granddaughter, Dorothy, who was married in 1939. Mary expended considerable time and patience finishing the edge of this quilt, so it may be assumed that she knew it was going on a four-poster bed similar to this authentic reproduction bird's-eye maple one. Appointments in most bedrooms were simple, with a colourful quilt such as this as the focal point.

Double Wedding Ring became one of the most popular designs during the 1930s and 1940s. People could not afford the luxuries of life, but they could create family treasures through the use of their scraps. These quilts were generally made as wedding gifts, therefore much care was taken in the choosing of the fabric and the execution of the piecing. It is a difficult design to piece accurately and great care must be taken in the cutting of the numerous shapes that comprise the design.

Certainly the quilt's owner, Ella Mann, would have had a well-stocked hope chest at the time of her marriage. However, with the arrival of children, more quilts were needed, so she had some quilters in the Vineland area make this Double Wedding Ring quilt.

Pattern designs cross many cultures. It is not known where this design originated, but it suddenly appeared in the early 1920s and has been a favourite design for wedding quilts and other special-occasion gifts ever since.

It is interesting to note that the rings on this quilt are almost perfect circles. Generally, the design is slightly elliptical and thinner, which gives more open area in the centre for elaborate quilting, if so desired. Since this was a bed quilt and intended for constant use, the quilting was kept simple and a large central open area was not important. The pattern name is a romantic one, and though Mennonites do not wear wedding rings, they still enjoy pondering the symbolism of the wedding ring as it relates to love and marriage.

Double Wedding Ring c. 1935, Essex, Ontario, Mary Elizabeth Hyland

Gertrude Merrick lived in Cleveland, Ohio, when she made this Dresden Plate. Here we see a secondary pattern centred over the intersection of four plate blocks. After Gertrude seamed all of her plates by machine, she appliquéd them to the centre circle, which probably had been machine-stitched to the muslin block. By the early twentieth century, life was improving for housewives in some parts of the country, and quilters could spend more time co-ordinating their scraps and designing colour schemes to fit the decor of the rooms in which the quilts would be used. In this quilt, the centres, crossed leaves and backing are all of the same fabric, and most likely this quilt would have been reversed periodically to keep fabrics from fading too quickly.

Gertrude quilted several concentric rings within each plate, as well as one in the centre of the leaf motif. Much care was taken with the quilting, as the stitching is uniform and particularly straight.

This quilt could certainly be used and enjoyed with either side up.

It is interesting to note that the secondary pattern is identical to the one used by Phyllis McQuade in her quilt on page 47.

Dresden Plate has long been a favourite design for quilters. Carol chose it for her first quilt. Her aunt Laura Bricker of Baden helped her with the design and construction. If you look carefully, you will see that the pencil lines marking the quilting design are still visible.

Two neighbouring Mennonite sisters, Barbara and Mattie Salzman of Baden, did the actual quilting, and Carol was allowed to go over and quilt on it whenever she wished. Generally, most Mennonite quilters do not worry about their pencil lines. They feel that with wear and washing the marks will ultimately fade to a point where they won't be so distracting. Carol, however, has cherished this quilt for many years and has not laundered it often, so the lines are still visible.

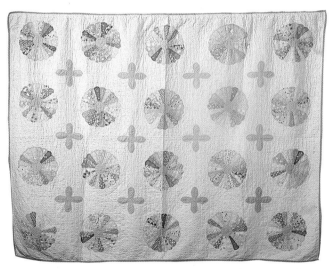

Dresden Plate Variation *c. 1920 Cleveland, Ohio, Gertrude Merrick*

Dresden Plate *1968, Baden, Ontario, Carol McLean*

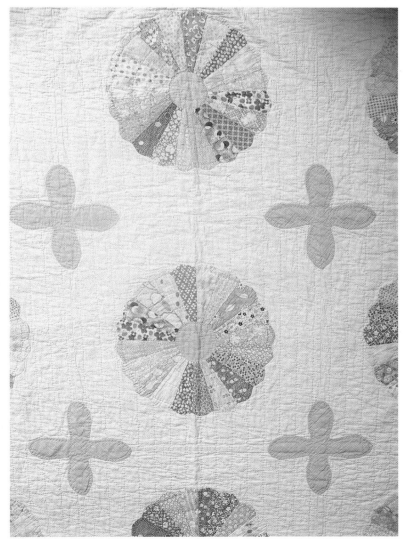

*Detail of **Dresden Plate** 1968*

BASKET QUILTS

Floral Bouquets, *origin unknown*

Baskets and flowers were important to farm women. The flowers in this quilt were created from an assortment of small-scale prints and ginghams, which make for a delicate design. The containers have been pieced from solid colours and create the illusion of flowerpots. The inspiration for this design could have come from wandering in the woods and picking dainty wildflowers similar to the ones growing along the slope in this photograph.

An overcast spring day is a perfect time to air quilts and prepare for summer by changing the quilts from the heavy woollen winter ones to light, cheery cotton ones. The flowers in this Scrap quilt are pieced triangles done in soft colours. This quilt was made for immediate family use, so no time was spent appliquéing flowers in the baskets.

Pieced Flower Baskets c. 1925, Mount Forest, Ontario, Eliza Evans

Herald and *Star Weekly*, both of which periodically published floral appliqué blocks. She made this quilt shortly after she was married in 1930. When it was time to quilt it, neighbours were invited over for a quilting bee.

Margaret McIlmoyle chose to make a simple Cherry Basket quilt as part of her trousseau, using several shades of pink fabric. Like baskets on a farm, where shape and size vary, so too do baskets on a quilt. Margaret's are larger than Laura's and are the only design element. As a trousseau quilt, this one was carefully made and quilted and was only used on the spare bed. Like Laura's, these quilts are in pristine condition and given the proper care should last for many years to come.

Flower Baskets c. 1936, Petrolia, Ontario, Laura Steadman
Cherry Baskets c. 1930, Selwyn, Ontario, Margaret McIlmoyle

Eliza Evans enjoyed piecing and made many styles of quilts during her lifetime. This two-colour Pieced Basket quilt was made for daily household use. Each basket was machine-pieced and the handles were carefully appliquéd onto the block. Each block was sashed for added interest and the whole surface of the quilt was quilted using the clamshell motif.

While the fabric was not home-dyed, the quilter did enjoy using colours that were found in nature. The daffodils in the pitcher reflect the same shade of burnt orange prevalent in many early quilts. Flowers and baskets were common items in any farm home and popular motifs in quilts.

Laura Steadman enjoyed her garden. It is assumed that she got these patterns from the *Family*

Colonial Basket *c. 1910*
Eastern Ontario
Pieced Baskets *c. 1880*
Fonthill, Ontario
Catherine Goring

Baskets, food and the land—
things familar to all farmers. Here
we see two different Basket variations made some 40 years apart.

The quilter who made the
Colonial Basket variation must
have lived on a fruit farm. These
baskets appear to be ready to hang
from a loaded cherry branch while
they are filled with the ripened
fruit. Often, in bygone years, the
shade of red used in these quilts
was referred to as "cherry red."
Red-and-white quilts have been a
favourite since quilting began.

The Pieced Basket variation
was all handpieced by Catherine
Goring, born in 1841. She was the
great-grandmother of its present
owner. The Goring family were
farmers in the Niagara Peninsula
and were familar with all the hard
work and planning required to be
successful fruit farmers.

Both of these quilts have thin
cotton batting and were quilted
with a simple diagonal grid.

CARE OF QUILTS

Proper care of any quilt will extend its life and beauty for many years. It is important that a quilt be carefully examined before embarking on any type of repair or cleaning. When examining a quilt, look for broken seams, frayed areas, broken quilting stitches and weak or rotting areas. Make notes on your findings and then examine the quilt again to try to identify the types of fabrics and the kind of batting used. It is not always easy to identify the fabrics, so if necessary seek expert help.

The cleaning of a quilt will depend on several factors: age, type of fabric, condition of quilt and type of construction. All of these factors must be evaluated before proceeding. You must also establish whether or not you are working on a "museum" piece or a functional bedcovering. If it is a museum piece, seek expert advice before you begin. It might also be prudent to obtain more than one opinion before launching into the cleaning of an antique quilt. When contemplating the care and cleaning of an antique quilt, it should be noted that an aged quilt *will* not and *should* not look pristine.

METHODS OF CLEANING

Vacuuming
This is the easiest and most effective way of removing loose soil from a quilt. If a quilt is sufficiently small, a gentle shake outside will dislodge loose dust particles; however, be careful not to snap the quilting stitches. Vacuuming should be done prior to any other type of cleaning. Brushing with a soft brush will also loosen and remove surface dust. Use only the soft brush of your vacuum after placing a piece of fine nylon screening over the textile. *Do not*

Nelson's Victory c. 1940, Bellville, Ontario, Deacon Sisters

drag the vacuum over a quilt. Hold it just above the surface. Procedure:
1. Lay the quilt on a clean table and cover it with nylon screening.
2. Use a low-suction hand-held vacuum with a small brush attachment. Slowly pass the vacuum over top of the quilt. Too much suction will suck the batting through the fibres of the top.
3. Turn back half of the quilt, vacuum the table and repeat the process for the other half.
4. Turn the quilt and repeat the procedure for the back.

Note: Vacuum slowly to remove the soil and also to be certain that the quilt is not sucked into the vacuum.

Airing
It is important that an attempt be made to air quilts once or twice a year. Since the increasingly polluted atmosphere and daylight have both proven to be damaging to aging fibres, I recommend that quilts be aired spread out inside your house or inside your garage. All old quilts should be aired flat so as not to stress the quilting stitches. A flat, well-ventilated surface can be made by using some type of screening (its rough edges covered with masking tape) supported by sawhorses. However, remember to cover the screening with a protective piece of fabric before placing your quilt on it. Leave the quilt to air for 2 to 3 hours.

Wet Cleaning
This can be very risky if you are not certain what types of fabrics are in the quilt or what type of batting has been used.

Before embarking on this type of cleaning, test each fabric first. Place a few drops of water on a patch and blot with a paper towel. If any colour runs, the quilt *cannot* be wet cleaned. Most, but not all, cotton quilts made after 1920 can be wet cleaned.

Remember, antique fabrics are very fragile when wet. Quilts should *never* be wrung. Water should be forced out of the quilt by pressing with your hands on the quilt and then blotting with bath or beach towels.

A bathtub is an excellent place to wash a quilt, if the quilt is not too large. However, before a wet quilt is removed from the tub, it must be supported. This can be accomplished by sliding a sturdy piece of plastic under the quilt. This piece of plastic, such as a carpet protector for use under office chairs, should be no larger than the interior of the bathtub, so that it can be slid under the quilt while it is in the tub.

First, soak the quilt in clean, *tepid* deionized or distilled water for about 10 minutes. Change the water once or twice. This will remove much of the dirt. If the quilt is very dirty, repeat this whole procedure.

Clean in an anionic detergent solution such as Orvus or WA paste, which are available at some quilt shops, drug or feed stores. Use about 2 tablespoons per bathtub of water and allow the quilt to soak about 10 minutes. Note: *Do not* use WA paste in the washing machine. Gently agitate the quilt in order to loosen the dirt particles. Wash a second time if required. If stains and spots remain on the quilt, they are best left alone, as old textiles can be damaged by further aggressive treatment.

Rinse several times in order to be certain that all traces of detergent have been removed. Let the quilt drain in the tub until most of the water is gone. You may apply some gentle hand pressure and then pat with large bath towels.

The best method of drying is to follow the same procedure as for airing. If drying indoors, use one or two fans on low speed to hasten the drying process. Change the fabric under the quilt (I suggest an old mattress pad) once, when the quilt is turned to dry the underside.

Any woollen quilt will have to be dry-cleaned, and it is suggested that you contact a historical museum in your area to see whom they recommend for such a delicate job. If you do not have an expert in your area, I suggest that you discuss the project with various dry cleaners or contact the Royal Ontario Museum in Toronto to see whom they would recommend.

INSECT INFESTATION

1. Place the quilt in 2 layers of polyethelene bags, in which you have also placed a packet of para-dichlorobenzene crystals wrapped in acid-free paper. *Be certain that crystals do not come into contact with the quilt.* For a 30-gallon bag, approximately ½ pound of crystals should be adequate. Make certain that the crystals are on top of the quilt, as vapours move downward.
2. Seal the bag with tape and leave it for 1 week. A temperature of 70°F is preferred.
3. Remove the quilt; vacuum and air it as directed earlier.
4. If the quilt can be laundered, this should remove any larvae.

MOLD

1. Allow the mold to dry and then vacuum it off.
2. Store your quilts in a dry environ-ment with good ventilation.

STORING

The easiest way to store a quilt is to lay it flat on a bed under your current display quilt. If you have a guest bed which is not in daily use, this is an easy method of storing a number of quilts. Once you have run out of beds, it then becomes important to consider alternative methods for storing your quilt treasures.

Quilts should never be stored in direct contact with unsealed wood or paper, as they contain acid which will react with the fabric. Acid-free cardboard cartons may be purchased for this purpose, as well as *unbuffered* acid-free paper. Buffered acid-free paper may contain alkalis which can damage many textiles, particularly wool and silk. Place the acid-free paper in the folds of a quilt.

When folding a quilt, it is best to fold it in one direction only, using the accordian pleating method, padding each fold with acid-free paper. This method takes extra time, but the stress on the fibres will be equally distributed front and back.

If you are making a wooden box in which to store your quilts, it is imperative that the wood be sealed. This may be accomplished by treating it with several coats of polyurethane.

Remember, never store quilts in plastic!

Another effective way of storing a quilt is to roll the quilt, pattern side out, on a tube or wooden dowel which has been sealed with polyurethane. Then, using at least 2 layers of acid-free tissue paper, roll the quilt around the tube (place the tube in line with either the warp or weft threads of the quilt). If the tube is long, 2 or more people should roll so as to maintain uniform tension. Wrap the rolled quilt with prewashed muslin (100-percent cotton), or better still with a well-used cotton flannel sheet, and tie it with strips of cotton. Place an identification label on the end of the tube. These tubes should then be suspended by both ends so that there is no weight on the quilt. An easy way to do this is to build several shelves of coated, grilled metal shelving and hang the quilts below the shelf by suspending the longest quilts the lowest and the shorter ones above.

All textiles should be stored away from light, heat and excessive humidity. The ideal environment is about 60°F with 50-percent humidity and good air circulation.

Air-conditioned homes are excellent environments for storing these family treasures. Hot attics and damp basements are the worst. Constant temperature and humidity year-round are important.

HANGING QUILTS FOR VIEWING PURPOSES

While we do wish to enjoy our quilts, we should be cognizant of the fact that light is the single most destructive enemy of fabric; hence, we should rotate our quilts every 3 or 4 months. Turn them over and enjoy the backs—many of the old quilts show beautiful quilting designs and stitching on their backs. Should you be hanging a quilt on the wall, there are a number of factors to consider.

Stress

Hanging a quilt will put a certain amount of stress on the fibres if it is not properly supported and rotated.

(a) If the quilt is of suitable size, a tubular sleeve may be sewn along the top of the back of the quilt. If the design is suitable, a sleeve may also be sewn on the bottom edge and then a board inserted to equalize distribution of stress; the quilt may then be turned periodically. If a quilt is square, it may be turned 45 degrees and the above procedure may be followed. Note: This puts the surface of the quilt under tension and should not be used for prolonged periods of time. When a tubular sleeve is used, the hanging device never comes in contact with the quilt, thus eliminating potential damage. A quilt longer than 48 inches should have the sleeve slit once or twice so that the hanging device may be supported by a wall bracket periodically.
(b) Some older and more fragile quilts should probably be supported on all sides. This

will involve the construction of a sleeve for each of the 4 sides of the quilt and a wooden frame the same size as the back of the quilt. To construct the sleeves for the 4 sides of the quilt proceed as follows:

1. Cut strips of Velcro 1 inch shorter in length than the measure of one side of the quilt.
2. Use cotton fabric to make a sleeve which, when completed and turned inside out, is ½ inch wider than the Velcro. Make the sleeve by cutting medium-weight muslin twice the required *width* plus 1 inch for the seam allowance by the *length* of the side of the quilt plus 1 inch. Fold the right sides together and seam with a ½-inch seam. Turn right side out and press. Turn the ends in so that the sleeve is the length of the Velcro and press.
3. Centre the looped side of the Velcro on the sleeve and attach by hand or machine-stitching along the selvage and across the two ends.

Figure 1

4. Cut a strip of ¼-inch-thick wood (dressed on both sides; i.e., planed and/or sanded) ½ inch wider than the Velcro. Seal the wood with acrylic latex paint or polyurethane and
attach the hooked piece of Velcro to this with staples at about 3-inch intervals along the 4 edges.
5. Repeat the above for the 4 sides.
6. Mitre the 4 corners of the frame together and adjust the Velcro on the quilt if necessary.
7. Insert screw-eyes at both ends of the wood on the top side of the frame.
8. Mount the prepared quilt to the frame by pressing together the hook and loop tapes of the Velcro (start at the centre and work out towards the ends of each side).
9. Mount the frame with the quilt

on the wall.

Figure 2.
While this is a time-consuming project, it is actually the best way to hang antique quilts, as it puts the least amount of stress on the fibres. A frame may be constructed so that it is easily collapsed and stored when not in use.

Blazing Star c. 1885, Steven's Point, Wisconsin, Mrs. Cartmill *Scrap,* origin unknown

QUILT PATTERNS

JACOB'S LADDER

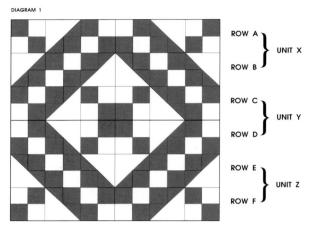

DIAGRAM 1

ROW A
ROW B
} UNIT X

ROW C
ROW D
} UNIT Y

ROW E
ROW F
} UNIT Z

Before you start to cut your fabric for this quilt, make several test blocks using one of the methods described below. This will assure that your finished blocks will be the desired size. Once you have established your cutting and seaming measurements, the cutting and sewing of this top will proceed very quickly.

Decide on the overall size of quilt you wish to make and then count the number of 4-patch and ½-square blocks you require. For each unit of 4 blocks you require the following: 20 4-patch blocks, 16 ½-square blocks.

As you can see, it takes *at least* 4 blocks set together to make the chain of colours emerge.

When you add the next unit of 4 blocks, you will see a large red square forming at each edge, just as the black square formed in the centre.

Instructions are written for a 4-inch block. Should you wish another size, alter the measurements accordingly.

Four-patch blocks are sewn using a current "stripping" technique. If you do not have a cutting board, acrylic ruler and rotary cutter, you will have to cut templates.

Note: All seam allowances are to be ¼ inch.

1. Check to see that the grain of the fabric is straight. If not, pull the fabric so that the grainline is straight. Straighten the top edge of the fabric by squaring and cutting with your acrylic ruler.

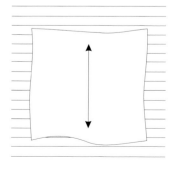

2. Cut a number of strips of the red and black fabric 2½ inches wide. The number of strips required will vary with the size of your quilt. Do a test unit and then decide on your finished size.

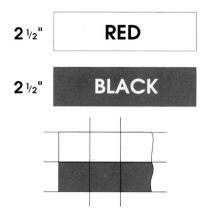

3. Sew a black strip to a red strip using a ¼-inch seam allowance.

4. Press the seam allowance to the darker fabric (i.e., the black fabric) so the seam allowance will not shadow through to the right side of the top.

5. Cut these strips into 2½-inch widths, making pieces 2½ x 4½ inches.

6. Sew 2 strips together to form a Four-patch block, being very careful to match the centre corners.

7. Press the seams to one side.

Half-Square Blocks

The best instructions for making these blocks are found in Barbara Johannah's *The Quick Quiltmaking Book*.
Make units that will be 4 inches on each side when finished.

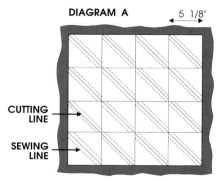

DIAGRAM A

5 1/8"

CUTTING LINE

SEWING LINE

1. Lay a piece of red fabric on top of a piece of black fabric and align grainlines. Grid as per diagram A. Pin these 2 layers of fabric together.

2. The squares on this diagram are 5⅛ inches on each side.

3. Use a ruler to draw diagonal lines through each square.

4. Sew a ¼-inch seam on either side of the diagonal line, stopping at the intersection of each vertical and horizontal line. Lift presser foot and continue to sew on the line in the next block. Repeat at each intersection until all squares have been sewn.

5. Cut out squares and then cut each square on the diagonal line.

DIAGRAM B

6. Open squares and press seam allowance to dark side.

DIAGRAM C

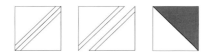

7. Trim corners of the diagonals.

TRIM BACK TO HERE

8. Check finished size of each square with an acrylic square designed for this purpose. They should measure 4½ inches.

9. Following Diagram 1, assemble blocks in rows.

10. Sew row A to row B, row C to row D and row E to row F.

11. Press seam allowances and seam unit X to unit Y to unit Z.

FRIENDSHIP CIRCLE

1. Graph block Z or copy it on a photostat machine and check for distortion. This should be a 3-inch block.

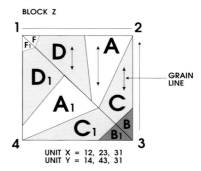

BLOCK Z

UNIT X = 12, 23, 31
UNIT Y = 14, 43, 31

Note: all (1) units are their matching template rotated or reversed. Therefore, you need only one set of templates, but you must be careful to cut on the straight of grain.

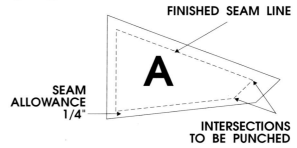

FINISHED SEAM LINE

SEAM ALLOWANCE 1/4"

INTERSECTIONS TO BE PUNCHED

2. Make templates A, B, C, D and F. When making these templates add ¼ inch to each side for seam allowance. Use sturdy material such as template plastic for these templates, as they will be used repeatedly.

3. To each template shape draw a finished seam line on each side. Take a sharp tool such as a thin finishing nail and pierce each template piece at the intersection of all seams.

Note: If you prefer to appliqué the octagonal shapes onto the intersection of the 4 blocks after they are sewn, draft the shape and allow sufficient seam allowance to turn under. Redraw template D to include shape F.

4. Observe that shapes C and D are background fabric and should all be cut from the same piece of fabric. Sort your scrap fabrics into piles to be used for shapes B, A and F.

5. Cut the fabrics and pile them according to template shapes.

6. Lay the template on the wrong side of each unit and using a sharp pencil mark seam intersections.

7. Assemble X units by sewing B to C, F to D, A to BC. Press the seam allowances to the dark fabric and then sew unit BCA to unit FD and press the seam allowance to the dark fabric. I suggest that you layer the seam allowances, as this will reduce the bulk for quilting.

8. Assemble unit Y in the same manner as unit X was assembled.

9. Sew X unit to Y unit to make a block Z.

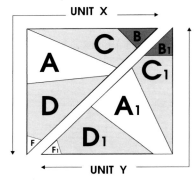

10. Check the block for accuracy, and square using an acrylic square that is marked for this purpose or make a template square which is 3½ by 3½ inches with ¼-inch seam allowance marked on all 4 sides.

11. When you have 20 or more blocks completed, sew 4 of them together to make the design. When assembling Z blocks to make an I block, you will take Z block and rotate it ¼ turn. Sew 2 together for the top and 2 together for the bottom. Then sew the 2 units together for a completed block I.

To Assemble Top

1. Decide on the width and length of the quilt.

2. Assemble blocks I in horizontal rows. Press the seam allowances in one direction for row 1 and in the opposite direction for row 2.

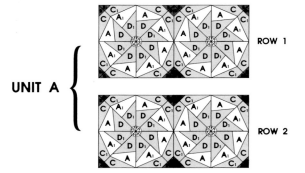

3. Sew row 1 to 2, 3 to 4. Continue until you have assembled all the rows.

4. Press the seam allowances in one direction.

5. Sew unit A to unit B and continue and press the seam allowances.

6. Repeat step 5 until the top is assembled.

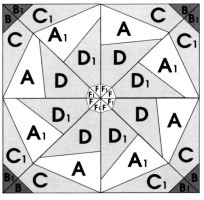

BLOCK I

To Prepare Top for Quilting

1. Be certain all the seam allowances are pressed and the excess bulk trimmed away.

2. Cut the backing about 4 inches wider and longer than the top.

3. Pin the backing onto the quilt frame *wrong* side up.

4. Centre the batting over the backing.

5. Centre the top over the batting *right* side up and pin to the quilt frame.

6. Pin the 3 layers carefully and then baste or pin them with safety pins about every 3 inches.

WREATH OF WILD ROSES - ADAPTATION

1. Decide on the size of your quilt. Study quilts in the book to determine whether or not you would like to border your design or finish it as was done with the quilt on page 84.
2. Draw the shapes on template material. I suggest you use template plastic, as the edges will not wear down.
   Note: The template size should be shaped to the solid line in the diagrams. The cutting line need *not* be marked. Cut about ⅛ inch away from the solid line to form your seam allowance which you will clip and turn under as required while appliquéing.
3. All the shapes will be marked on the *right* side of the fabric.
4. Shape B can be cut as a square about ½ inch larger than the circle. It will be placed under Shape A (red fabric). It will be applied using reverse appliqué techniques. See instruction #10.
5. Calculate the number of each unit required and cut them.
6. Cut the muslin blocks 14 x 14 inches. This will allow for shrinkage caused by appliquéing. As the blocks are completed or before assembling, square them off to 13½ x 13½ inches. Mark the grainline on the muslin before you cut the squares so that you can position the floral units appropriately, and the blocks will be assembled with the grainline running in only one direction.
7. Find the centre of each block by folding the block in ½ and then turning it ¼ turn and folding it in ½ again. Mark the centre with a small dot.
8. Position the design units symmetrically from the centre.
9. Position the stems first and sew in place using matching green thread and a small slipstitch.
10. Note: Floral unit is assembled before it is applied to the block. Position the template B(1) over the centre of unit A and trace around the solid line. Baste as per Diagram 2. Holding the orange fabric away from the red fabric, make a small cut along the cutting line, turn under along the solid line with the edge of your needle and slipstitch

in place with matching red thread. Continue to snip, turn and stitch until the circle is completed.
11. Position the floral unit over the stem and baste in position. Snip and needle-turn the edge under. Slip stitch with matching red thread. See Diagram 2.
12. Complete 4 floral units and then position the petals and attach them using the same technique as used for applying the floral unit.
13. When the required number of blocks are completed, assemble them in horizontal rows.

The quilting design may be as simple or complex as you wish. Mary Ann chose a simple leaf design which she quilted very densely. However, it takes an accomplished quilter to execute the small uniform stitches required for this design. A simple leaf design would be effective combined with some filler lines. Space them about ½ inch apart.

Binding a Quilt

I believe a double-fold bias-edge binding is preferable to a straight-of-the-grain binding. This offers longer wear along the edge.
1. Decide on the width of your binding. Double this measurement and add ¾ inch for seam allowances.
2. Measure all 4 sides of the quilt and square it off; i.e., opposite sides should have the same measurement. Round the corners with a gentle curve.
3. Baste the outside edges together to eliminate any pulling of the fabric.
4. Measure back the width of the binding less ¼ inch and draw a line. Do this for all 4 sides.
5. Pin the binding on the right side of the quilt along this line with the folded edge towards the centre of the quilt.
6. Sew ¼ inch from the raw edge. Ease the binding around the curved corners.
7. Fold the binding to the back and pin. Handstitch with a slip-stitch.

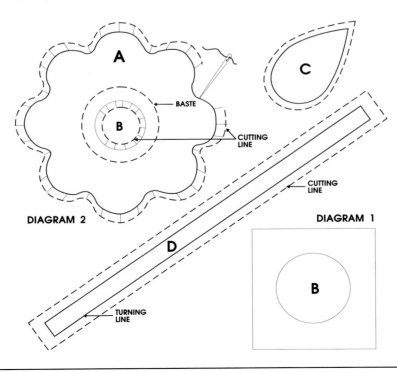

DIAGRAM 2

DIAGRAM 1

INDEX

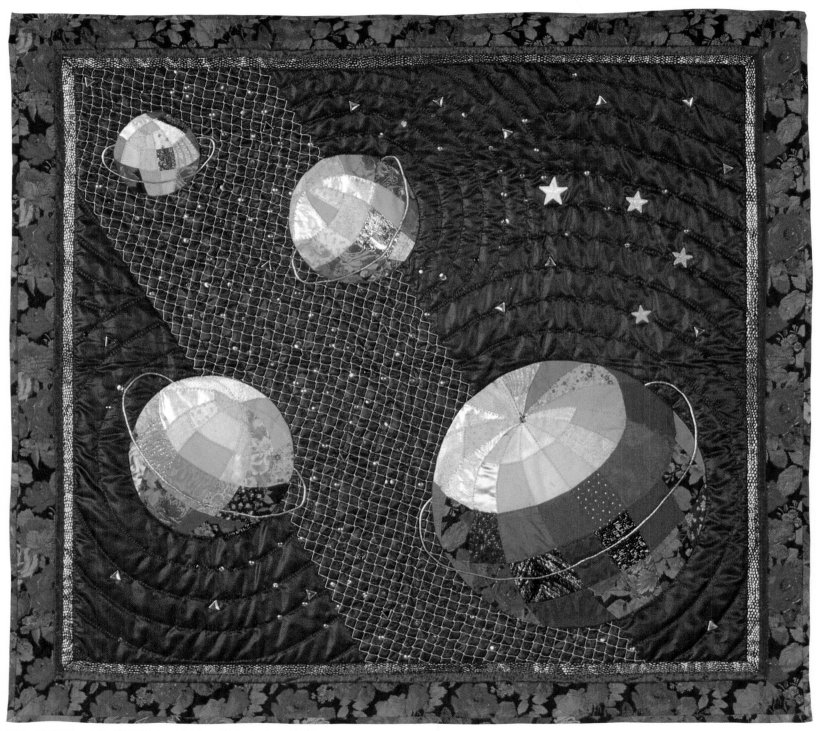

*"**World Without End"** 1990, Leamington, Ontario, June Dickin*
The title, "World Without End," is drawn from the biblical prayer. June's quilt humbly portrays the promises of the prayer and a joy in looking toward the future.